SOUTHWEST SAGA

—the way it really was!

by

WILLIAM C. McGAW

Golden West Publishers

Front and back cover designs by Bruce Fischer/The Art Studio

Library of Congress Cataloging-in-Publication Data

McGaw, William C. (William Cochran)
    Southwest saga: how it really was / by William C. McGaw.

    160 p. cm.
    Includes index.
    1. Southwest, New—History—1848—Anecdotes. 2. Southwest,
New—Biography—Anecdotes. I. Title.
F786.M48 1988   979—dc19   88-6078 CIP
ISBN 0-914846-35-3

Printed in the United States of America

Golden West Publishers
4113 N. Longview Ave.
Phoenix, AZ 85014, USA

Bill McGaw, author, on his favorite Appaloosa stallion,
War Dance, at his ranch near Mowry City, N.M.

Looking Backward for a Foreword

It has been my good fortune to spend the last thirty-five years living in—and traveling about—the Southwest, or that portion of it which includes West Texas, New Mexico, southern Colorado, Arizona, Nevada and the Mexican states of Sonora and Chihuahua.

I arrived on the scene in time to hold lengthy conversations with many of the **stars** of history in that region, and— fortunately—to establish eventually a trust and relationship with them that gave me an insight into the true history of the region.

In any country, or environment, at any time, there are many versions of both personal and historic events. Some are narrated to serve an ulterior motive, caprice or enlargement upon the truth, which brings us to the ancient question of:

What is truth?

Many observers care only slightly about what truth is, preferring to be entertained rather than accurately informed. This attitude is foreign to me because of my life-long training as a journalist, one of the lowest-paying professions in the world.

Its true reward, however, to those who hang in there long enough, is to uncover the real facts of any given time or situation. People with this desire to **set the record straight**, no matter what the cost, are rewarded by an enveloping joy which can be fully understood only by another person with the same obsession.

My career included working on major newspapers in Philadelphia, New York, Tampa, Miami, Indianapolis and a number of other places, during which time I built up an insatiable inquisitiveness into the nature of the singular and collective actions of mankind. Often the actual was different from the apparent, and there is no greater joy to the dedicated journalist or writer than to relate what truly occurred—and when, and why.

Sometimes the searcher's success is significant enough that he or she wins an award for the endeavor. This recognition, of course, is appreciated—I know for I have won several—but the **true** elation is in simply getting at the bottom of things when the rest of the world doesn't want to take the trouble, or perhaps is intentionally obfuscating the truth because of personal or monetary reasons.

I have researched each of the events related in this collection over a long period of years with whatever evidence still is available, often visiting with the people who made them happen, and eventually arriving at what I am convinced is the complete and unvarnished truth. The search itself is fun for the searcher, even if it ends in failure, or in a prolonged investigation without conclusion.

Thus, I am presenting what I have determined actually happened in each of the instances found between the covers of this book.

William C. McGaw

El Paso, Texas, 1988

Contents

CHAPTER I

Genesis

(Estevan's Life Among the Zunis)

The American Southwest was discovered in 1535 by four castaways, sole survivors of an expedition numbering about six hundred men who sailed from Spain on June 24, 1527.

Leader of the four was Cabeza de Vaca, who wrote an account of their adventures, known today as *Los Naufragios*, or *The Castaways*.[1] The other three were Alonzo del Castillo Maldonado, Andres Dorantes and the latter's servant, Estevanico, a black Moroccan.[2] They arrived at the present site of El Paso, Texas, in early December 1535, survivors of shipwrecks, Indian battles, and thousands of miles of walking after making it ashore at Galveston Island in November, 1528.

Following a number of disasters near Galveston, the survivors were reduced to nine, and five of these wandered off "and were driven to such extremity that they ate each other up, until only one remained, who—being left alone—there was nobody left to eat him."[3]

The remaining four continued walking westward for a number of years, living first with one tribe, then another, learning the languages of each. Dorantes' father was a physician in Spain and had passed on to his son the rudiments of healing. Dorantes, in turn, taught his companions the healing art and soon the Indians were calling them *shamen,* or medicine men, and were flocking to them for cures.

When they arrived in the El Paso area, hundreds of members of the Jumanos and Tigua tribes turned out to partake of physical cures. They bore a precious gift to reward the Spanish medicine men, too, a huge copper rattle cast in the likeness of a human head. Where did they get it? The Indians said it came from the north, where there was an abundance of this metal, indicating that the tribes up there possessed a copper foundry "of some complexity to cast copper in a hollow form."[4]

By this time, the Castaways had practiced medicine for a

number of years, becoming so adept that Cabeza de Vaca was surely the first to perform open-heart surgery in this part of the world. Near El Paso, de Vaca relates, "They brought me a man who—they said—a long time ago had been shot through the left side of the back with an arrow, the head of which stuck close to the heart. He said it gave him great pain and that on this account he was sick. I touched the region of the body and felt the arrowhead, and that it had pierced the cartilage. So, with a knife, I cut open the breast to this place. The arrow had gotten athwart, and was difficult to remove. By cutting deeper, and inserting the point of the knife, I got it out with great difficulty. It was very long. Then, with deer bone, according to my knowledge of surgery, I made two stitches. After I had extracted the arrow, they begged me for it, and they sent it further inland so that the people there might see it also."[5]

"On account of this cure," wrote de Vaca, "they made many dances and festivities, as is their custom. The next day, I cut the stitches, and the Indian was well. The cut I made only showed a scar like a line in the palm of the hand, and he said that he felt not the least pain."

Open-heart surgery performed in the Southwest 450 years ago may appear anachronistic today, but the Indians possessed other addictions and habits which appear equally so.

"In this country," writes de Vaca, "they make themselves drunk by a certain smoke for which they will give all they have." This narcotic affliction was *Canabis sativa*, or marijuana, smoked today in great quantities both in Mexico, where it originates, and in the United States.

As depraved as this seemed to de Vaca, it paled in comparison to another condition afflicting other Redmen: homosexuality.

"During the time I was among them," he wrote, "I saw something very repulsive, namely a man married to another man. Such are impotent and womanish beings who dress like women and perform the office of women, but use bow and arrow and carry big loads. We saw many of them among these Indians."

Color segregation also seems to have been practiced by these Indians. After traveling northwest from El Paso, then back south, they came upon another tribe, one which had segregated itself because its members were almost white.

"They were well built," wrote de Vaca, "of very good physique and whiter than any we had seen until then."[6]

Even though segregated, those with lighter skins apparently did not consider themselves either superior to or inferior, only different. They held Estevanico the Black in high regard, so much so that he was sent in advance to prepare for the coming of the others. Estevan picked up languages rapidly and could sing and dance, which allowed him to arrange an enthusiastic welcome for those who came after him. His role was almost exactly that of today's television entertainment as a prelude to business announcements.

Literally thousands of Indians welcomed them to each new area, most seeking treatment and faith cures for their ills, but many simply sold on the possibility of entertainment. Certainly today's TV networks would find it difficult to top de Vaca's performance of open-heart surgery with a flint knife and have the patient walking away while multitudes watched.

The various Indian tribes also had their assortment of con games, such as the tale they told the Spanish about a certain Seven Cities of Cibola, where—they said—the houses were made of alabaster, trimmed in gold, silver and turquoise, as well as their hinting that the backlands were full of portable wealth—all this to lure the Spaniards from place to place to enjoy their cures.

Then one day the Spaniards' attention was riveted upon a piece of jewelry worn by one of the visiting Indians: a necklace decorated with a pendant made from a Spanish belt-buckle, worn by an Indian on a thong around his neck and held in place by a Spanish horseshoe nail.[7]

Castillo Maldonado happened to spot this device at a place within what is now the state of Chihuahua and Cabeza de Vaca explained it this way:

"He (Maldonado) took it from the Indians and asked who had brought it. They answered that some men, with beards like ours, had come from Heaven to that river. They had horses, lances and swords and had lanced the Indians.

"As cautiously as possible, we inquired what had become of those men. They replied they had gone to sea, putting their lances in the water and going into it themselves, and that afterwards they saw them on top of the waves, moving on toward the sunset."

Cabeza and those with him recognized the men as being Spanish slavers, out capturing Indians and taking them to Culiacan, then to Mexico City, where they were taken as laborers. The Spaniards hastened to explain they were not at all interested in capturing slaves, that when they caught up with them they would direct the slavers not to kill Indians or make them slaves or do them harm. Of that the Indians were very glad.[8]

Cabeza de Vaca and his companions finally caught up with the slavers and arranged a truce between them and the Indians, then proceeded on to Mexico City. From there, de Vaca returned to Spain and Estevanico returned to Culiacan, there joining a party under the leadership of Friar Marcos de Niza as advance agent for an expedition searching for the Seven Cities of Cibola.

If Esteban should find the cities, examine them, and if he should find them to contain little of value he was to send back a runner with a small cross, about as big as a man's hand. If there was a good amount he was to send a cross two hands high, and if the place was very rich, he was to send back still a larger cross.

Within four days after arriving, Estevanico sent back a cross "as high as a man," according to de Niza's letter, which meant the wealth was fabulous. When de Niza learned of this, he rushed forward and found Cibola which lay just east of today's border between Arizona and New Mexico, where the Zuni reservation is now located.

Friar Marcos finally encountered one of Estevanico's companions and, according to de Marcos, the man "came in great fright, having his face and body covered with sweat" and showing great sadness. He said that within a day's journey of the cities of Cibola, Estevanico had sent ahead the copper rattle bearing the likeness of a man's head and that the messenger took along also a string of bells with one white and one red feather, as a token of safe conduct and that he had come in peace. The distraught messenger said when he presented the copper rattle and its accoutrements to the principal chief of Cibola, the chief examined it, saw the bells and threw the device to the ground in a rage.

Estevanico saw no importance to the chief's reaction and continued on, but was taken prisoner when he reached the first city of Cibola. He tried to run away the next day, but the huge black man was run down and killed. This version of Estevan's demise has been accepted for the last 450 years, but in recent time an American Indian artist, Woody Crumbo, has come upon an entirely different version of Estevan's adventure among the Zunis.

Woody was curator of the El Paso Art Museum until a few years ago, when he resigned that position to devote full time to his painting, subsequently returning to his Oklahoma reservation to rejoin his Kiowa tribe. Before he departed, however, he spent several days visiting with a Zuni friend who had just returned from a lengthy stay in Mexico.

"My Zuni friend told me that Estevanico was not killed," Woody explained. He quoted his Zuni friend as saying that Estevan had, indeed, tried to escape, but that the Zunis had run him down, brought him back to the pueblo, and there deposited him once more into a hogan, using it as a sort of prison quarters.

"To make sure he wouldn't try to run off again," explained Woody, "they cut off both of his feet."

Woody explained all of this was due to the high regard in which they held this remarkable black man, that they were not trying to torture him, but rather seeing to it that he remained with them and not try to run away. They placed Estevan flat on his back and worshipped him as a god.

"Estevan," explained Crumbo, "lived on among the Zunis for many years, finally dying an old, old sort of deity, without feet."[9]

1. Cabeza de Vaca, *La Relacion que Dio Alvar Nunez Cabeza de Vaca de lo Acaescido en las Indias en la Armada donde Yua Poz Governadez de Narbaez,* published at Zamora, Spain, 1542.

2. Fannie Bandelier, translation of de Vaca's account, published by A. S. Barnes & Co., N.Y., 1905, titled, The *Journey of Alvar Nunez Cabeza de Vaca.*

3. Bandelier, *Journey of Cabeza de Vaca,* pp. 63-5, fn. 65.

4. Cyclone Covey translation of de Vaca's *Adventures in the Unknown Interior of America,* U. of New Mexico Press, Albuquerque, 1984, p. 108.

5. Bandelier, translation, de Vaca's *Journey,* pp. 140-41.

6. Ibid., p. 133.

7. Ibid., pp. 161-2.

8. Ibid.

9. Woody Crumbo, interview with author, El Paso, 1967.

CHAPTER II

The Great Western Had Assets

(Warrior Woman of the Southwest)

Sarah Borginnis was every inch a soldier, and those inches were displayed in pleasant proportions, topped with honey-colored hair.

Few in General Zachary Taylor's army knew her true name, only that she was "The Great Western," a virago possessing consummate skills in both war and boudoir. She was awarded that pseudonym in tribute to her strength and bravery, awesomely demonstrated in at least two battles of the Mexican War. It also was an accolade to her towering beauty. Some grandiose, magnificent and powerful inventions of that era were christened "The Great Western," including the first steamship, an early railroad, and the finest champagne.

Precisely how Sarah came by this sobriquet is not recorded, but it is known the steamship that carried U.S. troops across the Gulf from New Orleans to the Mexican War was named "The Great Western." It was first related to Sarah in the *Niles Register*, a weekly news magazine, recounting a July 4, 1846, toast given in her honor by Lieutenant Braxton Bragg, before a group of Louisiana legislators at Matamoras, following Taylor's victory at Fort Brown.

Lieutenant Bragg's toast was proposed to "The Heroine of Fort Brown," and was reported in the *Niles Register* thus:

> In offering this toast, he (Bragg) said that during the whole bombardment the wife of one of the soldiers whose husband was ordered with the army to Point Isabel remained within the fort, and although the shot and shells were constantly flying on every side, she disdained to seek shelter in the bomb proofs, but labored the whole time cooking and taking care of the soldiers, without the least regard for her safety. Her bravery won the admiration of all who were in the fort, and she acquired the name of "The Great Western."

Sarah acquired other names and titles, too, during a career that extended from the early 1840s through the Civil War. She has been described in various journals, letters and reminiscences as an angel, a whore, a good cook, a tender nurse, a brave fighter and, in short, somebody they were always happy to see.

George Washington Trahern left Mississippi as a lad to become one of Taylor's first cowboys, or men who drove cattle used to feed the army. He later joined Taylor's regular army as a custodian of beef provisions, telling historian H. H. Bancroft:

"You can imagine how tall she was; she could stand flat-footed and drop those little sugar plums right into my mouth—that way. She was an immense woman, would whip 'most anybody in a rough and tumble fight. She was an American woman, always with Taylor's divisions."[1]

"The Great Western" became a heroine almost immediately, for she figures largely in Brantz Mayer's book, *The Mexican War,* published in 1847, while the war was still in progress. Wrote Mayer:

Every war produces its singular characters whose influence or example are not without their due effect upon the troops, and at the conclusion of these chapters, which are stained with blood and battle, it may not be useless to sketch...the deeds of a woman whose courageous spirit bore her through the trials of this bombardment, but whose masculine hardihood was softened by the gentleness of her female heart. Woman has everywhere her sphere of power over the rougher sex, but the woman of the camp must possess qualities to which their tender sisters of the saloon are utter strangers.

Some years ago in the southwest, a good soldier joined one of the regiments, with this tall and gaunt wife whose lofty figure and stalwart frame almost entitled her as much as her husband to a place in the ranks of the Gallant Seventh—unwilling to abandon her liege lord upon his enlistment, this industrious female was immediately employed as one of the laundresses, three of whom are required to wash for the soldiers at a price regulated by the council of officers. "The Great Western"—for by this sobriquet was she known to the army—arrived at Corpus Christi with her husband and up to the period of departure for the Rio Grande performed appropriate duties, keeping in addition a "mess" for the younger officers of the regiment. When the army advanced, the women, with some exceptions, were dispatched by sea to Point Isabel, while a few procured ponies to follow the soldiers in their tedious march. The husband of "The Great Western" was sent in one of the transports to the Brazos, but his hardy spouse did not deign to accompany him in this comfortable mode of transit, declaring "the boys of my mess must have some one to take care of them on their march."

Accordingly, having purchased a cart and loaded it with luggage, cooking utensils and supplies, she mounted behind her donkey with whip in hand, and displayed during the wearisome advance qualities which the best teamster in the train might have envied. Throughout the whole journey she kept her boarders well provided with excellent rations; and when her brigade reached the banks of the Colorado, she was one of the first who offered to cross in the face of the resisting enemy.

After calmly surveying the scene, which has been described, she remarked, with great coolness, that if the general would give her a pair of tongs, she would "wade the river and whip every scoundrel Mexican that dared to show his face on the opposite side."

When Taylor marched to Point Isabel on May 1, "The Great Western" was, of course, behind with the Seventh Infantry. Together with eight or ten women who remained, she moved at once into the fort, where her mess was soon re-established in a tent near the center of the works. The enemy's fire began on the third, as she was commencing her preparations for breakfast and the women were, of course, immediately deposited for safety in the almost vacant magazines. But it may be recorded to their honor that they were not idle during the siege. Nobly did they ply their needles in preparation of sandbags for the soldiers' and officers' tents, strengthening the works and protecting the artillerists whilst serving their guns; yet "The Great Western" declining either to sew or nestle in the magazine, continued her labors over the fire in the open air. After discharge of the first gun all were at their posts, answering the shot from the Mexican force; and, when the hour for breakfast arrived, none expected the luxury that awaited them. Nevertheless, the *mess* was well attended, as if nothing but a morning drill, with blank cartridges, had occurred, and, in addition a large supply of coffee awaited the thirsty, who had but to come and partake without distinction of rank.

To some of the artillerists who were unable to leave their guns, the beverage was carried by this excellent female; and as it may be readily believed, no belle of Orleans ever met a more gracious reception. The fire of artillery was kept up almost until near the dinner hour, when "The Great Western" again provided savory soup which she distributed to the men without charge.

Thus did she continue to fulfill her duties during the seven days bombardment. She was ever to be found at her post; her meals were always ready at the proper hour, and always of the best the camp afforded.

When dispatches, sent by Walker, were made up for General Taylor on the evening of the fourth, a number of officers and men wrote their friends at Point Isabel; and among them this courageous woman found time to communicate with her husband who had been dispatched from the depot. In this document she expressed her full confidence in the ability of the garrison to sustain itself, and only regretted the absence of her spouse. To supply his place, however,

Sarah Borginnis was known as "The Great Western" in the Southwest. She kept order in her own establishment, as this picture shows. It was painted by her friend Sam Chamberlain who saw her in action many times before and after 1850. This scene occurred in El Paso's first hotel, owned by Sarah.

she applied early in the action, for a musket and ammunition which she placed in security, expressing her determination to have full satisfaction whenever the enemy dared to approach within the range of her piece. This they never did, and our indomitable heroine must rest contented with the reflection that she nobly performed her duty, and will be long remembered by the besieged garrison, Fort Brown.

Sam Chamberlain, a member of the First Regiment of the U.S. Dragoons, wrote a book of his experiences in Mexico.[2] He describes Sarah as "a horsewoman who was recognized by all as Sarah Borginnis, the celebrated 'Great Western'."

Her infantryman husband was generally considered to have been killed in the early fighting near Point Isabel. Anyway, he dropped out of sight, and Sarah later went to Saltillo, Mexico, where she opened a place called the American House, described as a sort of hotel.

She operated this establishment until February 22, 1847, on which day she closed, but not in honor of George Washington's birthday. She and her staff were joining the troops in the field. Taylor, on February 20, had advanced on

Agua Nueva, 18 miles west of Saltillo, just as Mexican General Santa Ana reached Encarnacion, about 35 miles away, with some 20,000 men. Because of a poor defensive position, Taylor withdrew the next day to La Angostura, a mountain defile along the Saltillo-San Luis Potosi road, three miles north of the Hacienda Buena Vista. There his 4,800 untried U.S. Volunteers dug in.

This was the setting when "The Great Western" received news a battle was brewing.

Sarah closed her American House, loaded her girls into a wagon filled with camp kettles, blankets, sheets, mattresses, coffee and whiskey. They rattled down the trail and through Angostura Pass, halting in a tree-shaded area where Dr. Charles Hitchcock was setting up surgery. Here they put several gallons of coffee on to boil and were soon scrubbing amputation tables.

This chore finished, Sarah climbed to one of the highest points in the area—some 6,000 feet above sea-level—to watch 20,000 Mexican soldiers spread out across the plains of Buena Vista. They wore red, green and blue uniforms, set off with white belts and burnished brass.

Massed bands played a solemn mass anthem while a brigade of priests, archbishops and padres marched onto the field. The 14,000 infantrymen knelt, uncovered their heads, and 6,000 cavalrymen dipped lances as benediction was bestowed.[3] After mass, Santa Ana departed with General Ampudia, commander of four battalions of infantry.

Shortly before midnight, February 21, Colonel Yell's American troops were attacked by Ampudia's forces, which destroyed some stores, then they retreated toward Buena Vista, where they arrived at daybreak. Santa Ana thought the entire U.S. force was in retreat, so he sent terms of surrender under a truce flag to General Taylor. It was delivered by a German Army surgeon serving in the Mexican forces.

The German interpreted Santa Ana's missive thus:

"You are surrounded by twenty-thousand men, and cannon...avoid suffering a rout...but as you deserve consideration, I wish to save you from catastrophe and give notice you may surrender at discretion. You will be granted an hour to make up your mind." Signed: Ant. Lopez de Santa

Ana.

General Taylor replied: "Tell Santa Ana to go to hell! Major Bliss, put that in Spanish and send it back by this damned Dutchman."[4]

Fighting began at sun-up on the morning of February 23. "The Great Western" and Dutch Mary loaded wooden yokes on their shoulders and carried buckets of steaming coffee into battle. When the coffee gave out, they took as many of the wounded as they could assist and brought them to Dr. Hitchcock's field hospital.

About then the Second Indiana Battalion broke and ran, followed by the Arkansas Riflemen. The Second Illinois was out-flanked, so they, too, ran, leaving Captain John Paul Jones O'Brien and his artillerymen out in front, all by themselves. Without infantry protection, this position leaked Mexicans from all sides, so the Americans fell back with their three cannon still firing.

The enemy swarmed in, picked up one of O'Brien's cannons and began to walk away with it. General John Wool and his adjutant, Captain George Lincoln (a distant cousin of Congressman Abraham Lincoln) rallied the men of the Second Illinois and managed to turn the Arkansas boys around, too, but the Hoosiers kept running.

"The Great Western," tending the wounded, saw the Hoosiers racing off the field, with one especially terrified Hoosier in the lead. She dropped her bandages and headed off the cowardly soldier.

"Run for your life!" admonished the frightened man, just as Sarah got a grip on his jacket.

"Taylor is whipped!" he yelled. "The Great Western" swung him around, looked into his glazed eyes, then punched him in the nose.

"You miserable son-of-a-bitch!" Sarah screamed, "there ain't enough Mexicans in all of Mexico to whip old Taylor. You spread that report and I'll beat you to death."[5]

The retreating Hoosiers slowed down when they saw what happened, many stopping to watch the fight. They were impressed, so impressed, they turned and headed back into battle.

Jeff Davis arrived a short time later with his first Mississippi

Rifles (traveling in that swinging step peculiar to Indians and hunters). "The Great Western" shoved the cowardly Hoosier into the ranks of the Mississippians as they headed back into battle.

The returning Indiana troops and the Mississippians charged into more than a thousand Mexican cavalrymen trying to intercept the Americans. The astonished Mexican troops were mowed down with uncannily accurate rifle fire, then the Gringos tossed aside their rifles, clenched Bowie knives between their teeth (leaving their hands free) and grabbed the enemy mounts by the bits and pushed them back on their haunches. As the horses reared, most of the riders fell to the ground, then the Americans grabbed their knives and hacked them to pieces on the ground, as the Mexicans screamed: *"Diablos! Camisas Colorados!"* (Red-shirted devils!)

"The Great Western" and "Dutch Mary," meanwhile, had slung two more kettles of hot coffee across their shoulders and again strode into battle, Sarah with two pistols in her belt and Mary armed only with her wooden coffee dippers.

They drew abreast of Captain George Lincoln's Second Illinois just as the Mexican advance was stemmed. Lincoln, spotting the two women bearing the hot coffee, was so elated he whirled his white stallion about and yelled:

"Cheer up, boys! Lookee here—we got a lot to hurrah about. The ladies are on our side!"

Those were his last words, for at that moment a musketball slammed through his left side and his horse bolted, throwing the captain to the ground. When Dutch Mary reached him, Lincoln was already dead, and was smiling. The two women loaded the officer onto his horse and brought his body back to Dr. Hitchcock's field hospital.

The Americans did not know they had scored a victory until the sun rose over the Sierras the next morning. That was when the lookouts saw Santa Ana retreating towards Agua Nueva.

"The Great Western" helped load the wounded into wagons, then began the trek back down the road to Saltillo, where she converted her American House into a hospital. Later additional accommodations for the injured were found in the town's churches and public buildings.

One patient to recuperate at the American House was Colonel Samuel R. Curtis, a native of Wooster, Ohio, commander of the Third Regiment of Ohio Volunteers. Sam was not felled by a bullet, but by a vicious attack of malaria. He kept a journal,[6] and in it, wrote:

> Moved into the city and got a room at the American House kept by a woman who seems to be a part of the army. (Above the words "woman who seems," Sam wrote an interlinear notation, in a different ink, "Mrs. Boujitte," which may have been her name at this time.) She is nearly six feet high and well proportioned. She distinguished herself at Fort Brown during the bombardment in attending the sick and wounded and it is said to be a useful soldier. She has several servants, Negroes and Mexicans, and she knocks them about like children. While I am writing, she is watering her horse, a fine white horse that Lincoln was killed on."

An Austrian physician, Dr. Frederick A. Wisilizenus, stopped at Saltillo on May 23 and in his report, published as a U.S. Senate Document the next year, wrote:

> I stopped for some hours in the hotel of "The Great Western," kept by the celebrated vivandiere, honored with that *nom de guerre*, and whose fearless behavior during the Battle of Buena Vista was highly praised; she dressed many wounded soldiers on that day, and even carried them out of the thickest fight.

The doctor fails to give her name, but notes her occupation as *vivandiere*, a French word describing a woman who accompanies an army as a sutler, or one who sells food and drink. In reward for her bravery and services, she was commissioned a brevet colonel by General Winfield Scott.[7]

Diaries, letters and journals of this period kept by American fighting men give various spellings to her name, such as Bourdette, Bouget, Bourgett and Bourjitte, making it fairly likely that she subsequently married a man of similar name after the death of her first husband. In the census of 1860 for Socorro, N.M., the census taker listed the presence of a Sarah Bourgette, age 33, birthplace, Tennessee. She is known to have been in Socorro at about this time setting up a military hospital.

When the Mexican War ended, most of the enlisted men chose to continue westward for California, either in the service, or on their own.

Sam Chamberlain headed west with a small unit composed

of members of the First and Second Dragoons, accompanied by a battery of light artillery. This unit was commanded by Lieutenant Colonel John Washington.

According to Chamberlain,[8] the unit had been on the march for only a day or two when it camped at Palomas Pass, near Arista Mills, in the vicinity of Saltillo. There, before dark, a sentry observed three large freight wagons approach, led by "The Great Western," mounted on the white horse of the late Captain Lincoln and outfitted in a royal purple velvet riding habit, topped off with a cavalier's hat and white plume. She signalled her servants to halt and rode forward to greet her old friend, Colonel Washington.

"Colonel," she is quoted, "I request permission to accompany your detachment to California, which I hear has more to offer than does this bloody, trampled over desert."

Colonel Washington told her she must first marry a dragoon and be mustered in as a laundress. Sarah agreed, declaring, "I am always happy to serve. I'll marry the whole squadron, you thrown in, but what I go along."

She then spurred her mount up and down the line, crying out:

"Who wants a wife with $15,000?"

Portrait of Sarah Borginnis by Susan Ulmer, from sketches by Sam Chamberlain and descriptions by Sarah's contemporaries.

When there was no response, Sarah flounced her skirt, exposing lots of thigh, and added: ". . . and the biggest leg in Mexico. Don't all speak at once, now. Who will be the lucky man?"

An E. Company soldier stepped forward to say: "I have no objection to making you my wife, but only if there is a clergyman to tie the knot."

Sarah rode over to the volunteer, looked down and said, "Bring your blanket and yourself to my tent tonight and I reckon I will learn you how to tie a knot that will surely satisfy a lonesome soldier, such as you."

That consummated the marriage, according to Chamberlain, "in a howl of laughter."[9]

"The Great Western" never reached California, but remained in the Southwest for the balance of her life. After crossing the Sierra Madres, Washington's caravan arrived at the Bavispe River, where a group of scalp hunters were camped, performing what was for them the strange task of gathering and drying fruit, instead of scalps.

"With this party from New Mexico," explains Chamberlain, "was a man of remarkable size and strength. Madam Sarah Borginnis-Davis, "The Great Western," saw this Hercules while bathing and conceived a violent passion for him. She sought an interview, and with blushes told him of her love. The Samson, nothing loth, became a willing captive of this modern Delilah, who straightaway kicked Davis out of her affections and tent and established her lover in full possession without further ceremony."[10]

Lieutenant William Henry Whiting kept a diary, and on Thursday, April 12, 1849, he wrote that they met Sarah crossing the Rio Grande from old El Paso (today's Juarez, Mex.) to El Paso, Texas, of today. Whiting, who was a member of the Army Boundary Reconnaissance, wrote: "The first person we met, in a dugout, was the celebrated Great Western. Never has anyone been more delighted at the sight of American officers than she. Her masculine arms lifted us, one at a time, off our feet. She was about moving to the American side to await the coming of the army."

"The Great Western" then became involved in a partnership with Benjamin Franklin Coons, a Santa Fe trader from St. Louis. They formed a partnership to buy a property known as Ponce's Ranch, which was the original site of El Paso.

C. C. Cox arrived at Franklin on July 10, 1849, and found "The Great Western" was one of the first settlers at that place. Wrote Cox:

"That property on this side of the river (Rio Grande) was recently purchased by Mr. Coons, a trader from Missouri. He also has a large store. The other resident of this place is "The Great Western," a female notorious in the late war."[11]

Two other California-bound adventurers, Rip Ford and Lewis B. Harris, also encountered Sarah at the site of old El Paso. In his memoirs, Ford wrote: "On our side an American woman, known as "The Great Western," kept a hotel. She was very tall, large and well-made. She had a reputation of being something of the roughest fighter on the Rio Grande; and she was approached in a polite, if not humble, manner by all of us, the writer in particular."[12]

Harris, in a letter received by his brother in late August 1849, said:

"We found the far-famed Great Western at this place on our side of the river. She was celebrated in the Mexican War, and did good service in a number of battles. She is six-feet, one-inch in height, and well proportioned. She treated us with great kindness.[13]

By fall of 1849, part of the Ponce Ranch was leased to the U.S. Army (Fort Bliss) and Coons was advertising his fine hostelry, plus a commission and forwarding service, as well as a ferry service for merchandise or passengers across the Rio Grande. The hostelry was operated by "The Great Western" in 1849, but by the time of the 1850 census Sarah had moved with the army to Socorro, N.M., giving her age as 33, four years younger than she actually was.

Sarah's reason for shaving her age was perhaps because she was preparing to marry Sergeant Albert Bowman, who gave his age in the census as 24, and his birthplace Denmark. The marriage was apparently successful, for 10 years later, in 1860, they are listed as man and wife at Yuma, Arizona.

In 1851, Sarah and her new husband were moved to Fort Fillmore, near Mesilla, and in February 1852, she accompanied Major Samuel P. Heintzelman to Fort Yuma, where she established another army hospital, and opened another hotel and tavern, "on the bluffs."

· There is evidence also that Sarah was engaged in something more than a hospital or hotel business at Yuma. Lieutenant Sylvester Mowry arrived there in 1855 and wrote to his friend, Edward J. Bicknell, that he "had several virgins in training" from a local Indian tribe, and a letter to the same friend said, "We are surrounded by squaws all day long, entirely naked except for a little fringe of bark."[14]

Mowry wrote that female companionship in Yuma was cheap, that a pound of beads would buy a "tender moment" with 15 or 20 Indian maidens. He explained a pound of beads could be purchased for $2.50.

Mowry explained, also, that "The Great Western" could provide much better merchandise—young Mexican girls who were part Indian.

"Tonight," wrote Mowry, "is my wedding night. I have just got a Sonora girl for a mistress. She is 17, very pretty, dark hair, big black eyes and clear olive complexion."[15]

Sacks explained that "The Great Western" was not considered a procurer in the ordinary sense of the word, that "her kindly disposition caused her to take a number of young girls under her wing, not all of whom were by any means farmed out to pleasure-seeking lieutenants like Mowry."

When silver was discovered at Patagonia, Arizona, in 1857, Sarah set up a combination hotel, saloon and restaurant there also, and was well remembered by Jeff Ake, then an 11-year-old boy whose story was taken down by James B. O'Neil.[16]

O'Neil quotes Ake as saying: "At Patagonia I remember a woman who kept a saloon. They called her The Great Western. She packed two six-shooters, and they all said she sure could use them, that she had killed a couple of men in her time. She was a helluva good woman. I used to take eggs and stuff up for her to buy, and she would feed me. When the Civil War came and the soldiers moved out, she went with them to be near an army post. She was one of the first residents of Fort Yuma." She was also listed in the 1860 census as the wife of Albert J. Bowman, an upholsterer.

A Confederate sympathizer, Sarah moved the following

year to Mesilla, N.M., then a Confederate headquarters and a long hike from Yuma.

Jeff explained that even with Sarah's good qualities, his father called her "the greatest whore in the west," meant as a compliment. Anyway, Jeff said, she "sent her girls back to Mexico."[17]

The Confederate sympathizers began their long trek eastward to Mesilla, then Confederate headquarters, for the West, picking up Moses Carson, Kit's older brother, before heading out. Those with the wagon train expected to meet a Confederate military escort at La Cienega (today's Silver City) but when they arrived there, they learned the troops had already departed.

They then continued alone, carrying all they possessed. Ake's father had with him $80,000 in doubloons, plus a lot of valuable livestock. It is surmised "The Great Western" bore her life-savings, plus all her possessions, as well as those of her husband.

The total party—which numbered 47, including Sam Houston—were jumped by Indians at a pass near the New Mexico Mimbres River. Houston rode for help while the rest held off the attackers for many hours, until Houston returned with a Confederate Cavalry troop which immediately drove off the Indians.

The wagons were soon put in a train once more, inventory taken, and it was found little had been lost to the Indians. Jeff's father didn't lose a single one of his doubloons, estimated to be worth $15 each at that time. When the caravan reached Mesilla, Jeff's father bought land near Las Cruces, built a home on it, and the Ake family lived there until the spring of 1862, when the Confederate Army retreated once more, this time to Austin and San Antonio.

Accompanying them were Sam Houston and Sam Bean, older brother of Judge Roy Bean, later to be known as "all the law west of the Pecos." Bean's wife, Petra, was the daughter of Jim Kirker, this country's greatest Indian fighter, so she probably was not new to this danger.

Following Civil War hostilities, "The Great Western" returned to Yuma, dying there December 31, 1866. Sarah was buried with military honors, including a band, and her grave was the first to be dug on the northeast slope of a hill overlooking Fort Yuma.

This burial ground became neglected within the next several years, so bad that in August 1890, the Quartermaster's Department in Washington ordered all the bodies to be removed from there and reburied in the new cemetery at San Francisco, where "The Great Western's" marker remains today, right where she would have wanted it—surrounded by her "boys."

1. George Washington Trahern narrative, an unpublished manuscript in the Bancroft Library, University of California, Berkeley.

2. Samuel E. Chamberlain, *My Confession*, Harper, New York, 1956.

3. Details of the Battle of Buena Vista are taken from *Complete History of the Mexican War: Its Causes, Conduct and Consequences*, C. N. Brooks, Hutchinson & Seabold, Philadelphia and Baltimore, 1849.

4. Chamberlain, *My Confession*, p. 116.

5. "The Great Western's" quotes are taken from George Washington Trahern's unpublished narrative in the Bancroft Library, U. of California, Berkeley.

6. Colonel Samuel R. Curtis, unpublished journal, Bancroft Library, U. of California, Berkeley.

7. Note in Chamberlain's *My Confession*, p. 202, by Editor Roger Butterfield, who described her as "A noted camp-follower who won fame throughout the army for her bravery during the bombardment of Fort Brown, Texas, in 1846, and made cartridges for the army at Buena Vista. She was breveted a colonel for her services, by order of General Scott and made a pensioner of the government. After the war she kept a saloon in Yuma, where as Mrs. Bowman-Phillips, she was buried in 1866 with full military honors."

8. Chamberlain's *My Confession*, pp. 241-2-3.

9. Ibid.

10. Ibid. p. 256

11. C. C. Cox Diary, "From Texas to California," *Southwestern Historical Quarterly*, XXXIX (October 1925).

12. John S. Ford, *Rip Ford's Texas*, Edited by Stephen Oates (Austin) 1963, 119-26.

13. Bancroft Library, U. of California, Berkeley.

14. B. Sacks, "Sylvester Mowry, Artilleryman, Libertine and Entrepreneur," *The American West*, Vol. 1, No. 3, Summer, 1964, pp. 14-24.

15. Ibid, p. 17.

16. James B. O'Neil, *They Die But Once, The Story of a Tejano*, Knight, New York, 1935 pp. 29-30.

17. Ibid.

CHAPTER III
Southwest Was Once in Twain
(The Coke Scheme of Sam Clemens)

The United States paid France $12 million for what is known as the Louisiana Purchase, a tremendous bargain even though nobody knew for sure exactly what territory this added to the Southwest.

The deal was so vague that Vice President Aaron Burr saw a chance to make a few bucks. He drew a map of his own, drew a circle around much of it, went to London, and offered to sell Britain the part he had outlined for a half-million dollars.[1]

The British turned down his proposal, not because it was a crooked deal, but because the price was too high.

Next, Burr dug up an Irishman named Harman Blennerhasset who agreed to finance the take-over of Mexico and make Burr its emperor, but there was a catch. Blennerhasset insisted that he be Grand Chamberlain with more executive power than the emperor. This deal fell through for want of a second.[2]

James Wilkinson was Commanding General of the United States Army at that time. He was also governor of the Louisiana Territory and was also taking money secretly from Spain for special favors. Even so, all of this failed to provide him with enough working capital, so he agreed to work a deal with Burr to take over all of Mexico for themselves. Even though Mexico was a catholic country, their scheme had the blessing of the Catholic Bishop of New Orleans, as well as that of the Mother Superior of that city's Ursuline Convent.[3]

This conspiracy would have worked, too, if Wilkinson hadn't got cold feet and denounced Burr's plot to President Thomas Jefferson, who then offered a reward for Burr's apprehension. It was soon collected and Burr was tried in Richmond, Virginia, and found innocent. Burr, now well educated in how deals are made, went to New York City and built a huge fortune practicing law, then married a beautiful widow from France who claimed she had slept with both

George Washington and Napoleon Bonaparte. Not on the same night, however.[4]

As a culmination of these and other interesting events, Missouri became a state and attracted another lawyer to move there from Tennessee. He was John Marshall Clemens, from Tennessee, and his fourth child was Samuel Langhorne Clemens, destined to become Mark Twain. Sam's father died when Sam was only 12, so he dropped out of school to learn the printer's trade from his brother, Orion, ending up in Keokuk, Iowa, where Orion published a newspaper and city directory.[5]

There Clemens read a book that changed his life, titled *Exploration of the Amazon,* by a U.S. Navy lieutenant.[6] From it, Clemens learned about a South American plant called coca, which produced a light green leaf possessing miraculous powers.

"Herndon told astonishing tales about coca," Twain recalled later, "a vegetable product of miraculous powers... so nourishing and so strength-giving that a native of the mountains would tramp all day up hill and down with a pinch of powdered coca and require no other sustenance. I was fired with a longing to open up a coca trade with all the world. During months I dreamed that dream and tried to contrive ways to get to Para (Brazil) and spring that splendid enterprise upon an unsuspecting planet."[7]

Sam had friends in Keokuk who also knew about coca. One was a physician, Dr. James Martin; the other a pharmacist, J. L. G. Ward. These three formed a company to market cocaine throughout the world and become rich. Even today the literary establishment doesn't know the difference between cocoa and coca, or has deliberately covered up evidence that Sam Clemens masterminded a scheme to make a fortune in the international drug trade—and that was well over a hundred years ago.

Clemens saw himself as benefactor of the working classes. He was convinced coca would prove a boon to the budding industrial age, that coca would reduce fatigue and curtail hunger, while making workers happier with their lot. There was growing evidence the laboring classes were in trouble, a theme hammered home in Charles Dana's New York *Tribune,* whose highest paid European correspondent was then Karl Marx.

Sam was then only 21 in a burgeoning world. By the time he reached Keokuk it had approached its zenith, booming sufficiently to make people hope they would die wealthy. After reading Herndon's book, he talked it over with his friends, Ward and Dr. Martin, and they agreed it would be a splendid idea to make their fortunes in a product that would ease the plight of the laboring class throughout the world. It would keep the workers happy and healthy.

The idea was so good, in fact, that a rival group in Keokuk heard about it and also planned, secretly, to get into the same business. The leader of this rival group was R. B. Ogden, who owned the building in which Orion Clemens' print shop was located. How Ogden got wind of Sam's idea is not clear, but Dr. Martin taught in a Keokuk medical college founded by Dr. J. F. Sanford and an Englishman, Dr. E. C. Francis, who joined with a banker, George Anderson, to form the rival group preparing to sell cocaine throughout the world.

Drs. Sanford, Francis and banker Anderson met while Sam and his friends were planning their coca company, and Anderson agreed to loan Sam's rivals $10,000 at 10 percent per year, to fund an expedition by Dr. Francis and a Des Moines business man named William Moore to South America to set up a cocaine company.[8]

This organizational meeting was held in August 1856, and Dr. Francis and Moore prepared to depart Keokuk for South America in September, for which an additional note for $3,000 was signed with Banker Anderson to pay Moore's expenses.

Dr. Francis tried to keep the true purpose of their trip a secret from Clemens and his medical friends, announcing to the press they were going to South America "to capture a condor," a huge vulture found in the Andes. When investors were asked why they would put up $13,000 for a stuffed bird, Dr. Francis said it was because it would "bring honor to the city."[9]

Co-signers on the note must have had some doubts, too, for when it came time for Francis and Moore to depart, they suggested that Dr. Francis obtain a $10,000 insurance policy on his life. To this he agreed.

Sam and his group were unaware they had competition. Dr. Martin and Pharmacist Ward raised their expense money personally, and left for Para, Brazil, but Sam was having trouble digging up sufficient cash.[10]

Sam's letter reveals Ward and Martin had already departed for South America, and that Sam was hoping to leave in mid-September. He couldn't raise the cash, however, and then an unbelievable thing happened, according to the story Mark Twain told his biographer, Albert Bigelow Paine.[11]

"It was an early day in November—bleak, bitter and gusty, with curling snow; most persons were indoors. Samuel Clemens, going down Main Street, saw a flying bit of paper pass him and he captured it. It was a fifty-dollar bill. He had never seen one before, but he recognized it. He thought he must be dreaming. In the end he could advertise his find."

Paine quoted Sam as saying, "I couldn't stand it any longer...I felt I must take the money and depart."

Mark Twain, as he looked about the time he tried to launch his coca business.

Indeed, an unlikely story, but anyway Clemens departed for Cincinnati, where he worked for a spell as a printer, then departed for New Orleans on the river steamer, "Paul Jones". But Dr. Francis and Moore reached New Orleans long before Sam did. The *Delta,* a New Orleans newspaper, carried a story of their arrival October 18, 1856, "preparatory to starting a voyage of scientific discovery to South America." There was no hint they planned to open cocaine traffic to the world, nor that they hoped to capture and stuff a condor.

"These gentlemen," explained the *Delta,* "are well known to this community as being able, scientific men, and we may expect some new and interesting facts about their labors." While in New Orleans, Dr. Francis did, indeed, take out a $10,000 policy on his life, naming the co-signers on the note as his beneficiaries. He left the policy in the hands of an old friend residing in New Orleans.

Dr. Francis and Moore then sailed for Caracas, Venezuela, shortly thereafter, months before Clemens finally arrived in New Orleans, only to learn there was no vessel scheduled to depart New Orleans for Para, Brazil, in the foreseeable future.

Sam then managed to get a job as an apprentice pilot to pilot Horace Bixby, with whom he had become friends on his way down the river. The fee was $100, which Sam borrowed from his sister, Pamela, when they reached St. Louis. Sam paid it over to Bixby upon reaching that city.

Nothing more was heard from Francis and Moore for a year, or so. Dr. Martin and his friend Ward seemed to have disappeared. Their names were removed from the 1857 edition of Orion Clemens' Keokuk directory. There is no evidence they reached Para, either, but they did depart Keokuk, definitely.

There was news about Dr. Francis and Moore, however, and it shocked Robert Ogden, who came down to the dining room from his apartment in the New York Metropolitan Hotel on the morning of September 14, 1857, for breakfast. He picked up the New York *Herald* and his attention was attracted to a headline: KILLED IN DUEL.

The story was from Caracas, Venezuela, and it told how two gentlemen described only as "Dr. Francis and William

Moore, both of Iowa," fought a duel and that "Dr. Francis was killed at first fire."

Ogden rushed back to Keokuk immediately and met with an unhappy group of co-signers on the $13,000 notes. These men were not at all pleased when he told them he didn't think the life insurance policy on the life of Dr. Francis would remain in force because dueling was usually ruled out as a proper cause of demise. This proved to be true when the policy was retrieved from Dr. Francis' friend residing in New Orleans.[12]

The case was turned over to a young attorney, John W. Noble, later to become a Civil War hero and a member of President Harrison's cabinet. Noble apparently already had connections strong enough with the Department of State to get our minister to Venezuela to approach that government for a ruling on the death and was handed an official opinion stating: "Dr. Francis died by accident." This obliged the insurance company to pay off.

Twain left no record of his part in the affair, nor did he ever say what happened to his friends Dr. Martin and pharmacist Ward, but the literary establishment has always referred to the proposed business as one involving the distribution of cocoa, not cocaine.

Typical is a story appearing in the Kansas City *Star*, March 21, 1926, telling of Sam's love affair with Annie Elizabeth Taylor, 17, at Keokuk. The account is based on two letters from Sam addressed to Annie and written while Clemens was waiting in New Orleans for Ward and Martin so they could ship out together for Brazil and make their fortune.

The *Star* explained the reason for Sam's wishing to go to Brazil: "A book on the upper Amazon," the *Star* related, "by Lieutenant Herndon had fired Sam Clemens with a desire to go to the headwaters of that great South American river, the Amazon, there to collect cocoa and make a fortune."

There they go again with that cocoa.

1. Samuel Eliot Morison, *Oxford History of the American People,* Oxford Press, New York, 1965, pp. 368-9.
2. Ibid.
3. Ibid.
4. Ibid. p. 370; also J. Thomas, *Universal Biography*, Lippincott, Philadelphia, 1871, p. 1300.

5. Albert Bigelow Paine, *Mark Twain, a Biography,* 3 vols. Harper & Bros., N.Y., Vol. 1, pp. 12-107.

6. William Lewis Herndon, *Exploration of the Amazon,* published by order of Congress, 1853.

7. Twain, *What is Man and Other Essays,* Harpers, N.Y., 1906.

8. Dorothy Pickett, *Keokuk Confidential, The Daily Gate City* newspaper, Keokuk, Iowa, Jan. 5, 1963.

9. Ibid.

10. Letter, S. L. Clemens to brother, Henry, Aug. 12, 1856, Keokuk, original in Vassar College Library, photocopy supplied by Francis Goudy, Special Collections Librarian.

11. Paine, Mark Twain *Biography,* Vol. 1, pp. 110-11.

12. *Keokuk Confidential,* Dorothy Pickett, *Daily Gate City,* Jan. 5, 1963.

CHAPTER IV
Diamonds Are A Town's Best Friend
(New Mexico Gem Rush)

Confederate sympathizers were numerous in the Southwest at the outset of the Civil War.

Lieutenant-Colonel John R. Baylor and the CSA Second Mounted Rifles occupied El Paso's Fort Bliss without Union resistance in July 1861. A few days later, Baylor took over the little town of La Mesilla and nearby Fort Fillmore.[1]

Major H. S. Sibley was made a Confederate Brigadier General with orders to organize a brigade at San Antonio for the formal invasion of New Mexico Territory. This unit, two-and-one-half-regiments, began marching west in November 1861, at the precise time Colonel E. R. S. Canby, Union Commander of the Department of New Mexico, was complaining to Washington that he was paralyzed for want of funds, that his men had not been paid in a year.[2]

At the outbreak of the war, most of the Union Army of the West was in California because that is where the gold was. A segment of that force, under the command of General James H. Carlton, marched eastward over high mountains and hot deserts in an attempt to keep the New Mexico Territory in the Union. It was suspected New Mexico had gold, and surely silver and copper. It was even rumored diamonds could be picked up off the desert floor in some places.

One of Carlton's stops that summer was at a place called Mexican Springs, about a hundred miles west of El Paso, and it would later become famous or infamous under a number of different names, such as Pyramid Station, Grant, Ralston City, and finally Shakespeare, its name today.

Almost at the same time a Norwegian sailor retired and came to the Southwest to see if he couldn't make a fortune, perhaps pick up a little gold or a few loose diamonds. He took a job with the Southern Overland Mail and Express Company and was sent to Mexican Springs as station agent. The Express Company changed the name of the stop to Pyramid

Station, after a nearby mountain called Pyramid.

By whatever name, the town consisted of one large adobe building, which served as a station stop and a residence for the Norwegian agent, named Johnny Evensen. In 1867, General U. S. Grant was at the peak of his popularity and the company re-named the station Grant, which it remained for about two years.

In 1869, a Yorkshire Englishman named Brown arrived at Grant, on his way to San Francisco. He got out of the coach to stretch his legs while Johnny changed horses and didn't return in time to continue on that stage. Johnny told him he'd find him a place on a coach arriving the next day, but Mr. Brown postponed his departure for several days after that.

Brown departed each morning, wearing a bowler hat, and walked usually toward the Burro Mountains, where he roamed up and down, studying the rock, sand and earthen formations. He would return at about dusk each evening and would say something like, "You have here an interesting geological formation."

A few days later a huge Scott named McPherson arrived by coach and also chose to spend some time. The two formed a team to walk about and discuss the "geological" formations of the area, so much so that Evenson began calling the Englishman Geological Brown.[3]

One day the two returned with a large bag of rocks and Brown put McPherson on the next stage out for San Francisco with instructions to report there to Brown's friend, George D. Roberts.

McPherson stopped over at Tucson and while there had a chat with the editor of the *Weekly Arizonan.* The next day that paper carried a story about almost pure silver ore McPherson was carrying to San Francisco, explaining that it came from a location so rich in metal that he "pried out masses of almost pure silver."[4]

A few days after the departure of McPherson, two more men showed up in Grant, both named Brown, thus making it the first municipality where three-quarters of the population was named Brown.

One of the newcomers introduced himself as W. B. Brown, a government surveyor who was so close-mouthed that

The Grant House was once Shakespeare's leading hotel, named after the Union general and President of the United States.

Adjacent to the Grant House, of course, was the saloon.

Evensen called him Dumb Brown. He was followed by an assayer, F. R. Brown, and when he was introduced to Evensen, the latter explained the other Browns had nicknames and what would he like to be called?

The third Brown hesitated for a moment, then replied, "I am simple Brown," and was so flustered he used the adjectival, rather than the adverbial form. In this confusion, he became Simple Brown.

Thus for a few days three-fourths of the people in Grant were named Geological, Dumb and Simple Brown.

It is certain Geological Brown was neither Dumb nor Simple when he directed McPherson to take the ore samples to George D. Roberts, a close friend of William C. Ralston, a San Francisco millionaire banker and financier who was impressed by the ore samples and agreed to finance the speculation at Grant. This, of course, led to another change of name: from Grant to Ralston City.

Shortly thereafter two more gentlemen arrived to examine the various mining locations. They were Asbury Harpending and M. Philip Arnold, both from Kentucky. Arnold examined the locations, then took off hurriedly for London. The British press soon quoted him as saying he had located some precious metals and interested some English interests in purchasing mining property.

Mining locations and townsites sold rapidly and people flocked to Ralston City from everywhere, as close as Tucson, as distant as London. Much of the town of Tucson had moved to Ralston by April 1870.[5] These newcomers, however, numerous as they were, formed only a small part of the influx of people who flocked there to get rich, either with a mining claim or in real estate, or in some other handy business. Ralston City enjoyed a remarkable boom—until, that is, it was discovered that Geological Brown should have spent more time on his geography.

Brown filed both mining and real estate claims in the wrong place. Ralston lay in the territory of New Mexico, not Arizona, so the land claims should have been filed at Pinos Altos, New Mexico, not Tucson, which was closer in miles, but in a different territory. This meant the Ralston-Roberts-Brown & Co., was selling land and rights to settlers and prospectors swarming into New Mexico, a territory in which the company had no claim or title. This, of course, caused considerable controversy "to develop between the miners and settlers over claims and titles."[6]

Land titles and other such details were eventually settled, but by autumn the mining and land selling schemes were slowing down to the point of unprofitability. Something was needed to juice up the boom. It was found in the Burro Mountains by M. Philip Arnold: Diamonds!

Carrying some of what they professed to be precious stones, Arnold and his assistant, a Mr. Cowper, departed for San Francisco, stopping off at Tucson just long enough to call on the editor of the *Citizen,* who wrote a story about how they were loaded down with bullion from the Ralston mines, but added: "They are also bringing specimens of crystals which they believe to be diamonds found in the mines. Mr. Cowper is sanguine they are genuine by comparison tests made of these with some Brazilian gems in his possession. He is quite sure rubies are also plentiful and other precious stones lying around inviting gatherers."[7]

They sold off the Burro Mines in London to an optimistic group, which provided operating capital for a gigantic diamond deal conceived and executed by Harpending, the Kentuckian, who announced he was making a quick trip to Holland. He then returned so secretly no details of his movements are available.

Harpending contended he knew nothing of any American diamond fields until he arrived back in this country in May 1872. However, a few years ago most of Harpending's personal papers came into the possession of a California stamp dealer, who turned them over to the California Historical Society.

They reveal a contract between Arnold and Harpending, outlining ownership of numerous diamonds and stipulating financial arrangements for a project in which they were jointly interested. It is dated October 1871, indicating Harpending was in this country at least six months before he acknowledged he was.

Arnold and an associate named Slack sauntered into the office of George D. Roberts in San Francisco one day and asked innocently if they might leave a bag full of diamonds in Roberts' vault for safe-keeping. After the prospectors departed, Roberts rushed to the office of William Ralston at the nearby Bank of California to ask if he might keep the diamonds in his vault. Roberts explained he didn't feel safe with such a fortune in stones within his own establishment.

Roberts told how these two prospectors had come across a diamond field someplace, but wouldn't even hint at where it was. Ralston doubted the authenticity of the stones, suggesting it would be a good idea to learn if the gems were genuine. The prospectors agreed this could be done. A few of the specimens were sent off to Tiffany's in New York for appraisal.

Word came back from Tiffany's that the diamonds were indeed diamonds, worth about $125,000, meaning the stones in Ralston's vault were worth more than a million dollars.

This spurred banker Ralston into a fury of action. He called in the two prospectors and explained how it would take a fortune to gather in diamonds from their field, have them cut and then exploit the market properly. Ralston estimated it could take as much as $12 million. He doubted the prospectors could raise this amount, and they agreed.

Ralston then offered his quick solution: He would give them a fast profit by paying them immediately $600,000 for the stones and the claim upon the property from which the gems came, provided they would lead him to the field immediately.

The two old gents conferred briefly, then came back with a counter: Pay them $660,000, half down immediately and the other half when they had led Ralston, or his representative, to the site. It was so agreed.

Ralston estimated the initial preliminaries would take at least a million dollars and that it was sure untold fortune lay farther down the line, so he called together a group of cronies to provide up-front money, form a diamond company, an immediate committee to lay the groundwork and start moving.

The committee list reads like a Who's Who of that day: Generals B. F. Butler and George B. McClellan, Horace Greeley, William S. Lent, Thomas Selby, George S. Dodge, William Willis, George D. Colton, Maurice Dore, Louis Sloss, W. F. Babcock, Samuel L. Barlow, and a representative from the prestigious House of Rothschild, a Mr. A. Gansi.

By providing the first million dollars, this select few earned the exclusive privilege to invest more money in a $10 million corporation to operate the business. Ralston predicted the operation would produce "about one million dollars worth of gems each month."

Ralston appointed Roberts to accompany investors (or their representatives) to the field for on-the-spot investigations with Henry Janin, a foremost authority who was a "tough customer" when it came to sniffing out far-fetched schemes.

California and much of the rest of the world was soon gripped by diamond fever. Newspapers in many languages told of the $10 million mining concern Ralston was forming. Stories were revived about how Kit Carson found rubies in Arizona a few years earlier. These increased the credibility of finding gems other than diamonds in Southwest fields.

Many soon concluded the diamond fields were within a day's journey of Ralston City, which was swamped with people, but after they arrived, the seekers didn't know quite what to do, nor where to search. This helped Ralston City business, which was already thriving. Four new saloons opened. A dozen new houses went up.

Johnny Evensen even got some competition in the stage-coach business, which was thriving. Starting on July 5, 1873, the weekly *Arizonan* began running ads telling of the J. F. Bennet & Co. Southern Mail & Express Co. which was running "a 2 horse vehicle 3 times a week from Tucson to the Burro mines, where they could contact with coaches for all parts of the U.S."

Predictions were made that Ralston and San Francisco, not Holland, would be the center of the lapidary trade. Investors from all over begged to be let in on the ground floor of the American diamond and precious gem business.

Ralston City was certain an additional $10 million would be subscribed in a single day, once the report verified the field's authenticity.

On August 12, 1872, the Albuquerque *Review* claimed diamond fever was raging not only from there to the Pacific slopes, but on the Eastern seaboard as well, so enthusiasm was at its peak when Janin, the expert, and Ralston's

Clarence King on Fortieth Parallel Survey, camped near Salt Lake City, October 1868.

investors reached the diamond field. San Francisco waited anxiously.

When the inspection was completed and the fields were pronounced a "wonderful discovery" by the *Alta California* newspaper, August 10, 1872, ecstasy broke out again. The newspaper said Janin had inspected the secret diamond fields and from one-and-a-half tons of gravel had washed out "more than a thousand diamonds, four pounds of rubies and dozens of sapphires." Janin then filed an official claim on 3,000 acres for the Ralston Combine.[8]

Clarence King, considered the foremost geologist in the U.S., read the "wonderful" story in the *Alta California* with trepidation. Much of the excitement resulted from a series King had done for *Atlantic* magazine and later made into a book. Because of his reputation, King was asked privately by potential investors what he thought of Ralston's multi-million dollar corporation. King had no opportunity to study Janin's reports until October, while on a train to San Francisco. After reaching this destination, he reviewed other meagre clues, then after a period of study, he wrote:

"I know from the condition of the Snake, Bear and Green rivers. . . at that time unfordable, that the diamond party with Roberts had not gone to Arizona, as alleged, and from the report of Janin I had learned that the discoveries had been made upon a mesa near pine timber. From knowledge of that country which answered the description, and. . . that place must lay within the limits of the Fortieth Parallel Survey."[9]

When King met with his associates the next morning, he told them he was convinced the diamond fields were not in the Ralston City area, as generally believed, nor in Arizona or New Mexico. King thought internal evidence in Janin's report implied the field lay in Colorado.[10]

From detailed knowledge and total recall of the geological formations in Colorado, King surmised the area inspected by Janin must be located in the tertiary beds of Vermillion Basin, near Brown's Park Mountains, site of today's Dinosaur National Monument, between the fortieth and forty-first parallel.

King then instructed his associate, James Gardiner, to remain in San Francisco to complete the atlas upon which they had been working. Then he reported to the War Department he was planning survey work on "carboniferous fossils," knowing nobody in the War Department had the brains to deduce such fossils were diamonds. He thus kept the movements of his group secret, and to further allay suspicion, they did not all depart at once, but took trains from different points.

King reached the southwest corner of Wyoming on October 28, and hit the trail four days later. They reached a western Colorado mesa on which a geodetic station was maintained and pitched camp. The next morning, King and Samuel Emmons rode down the gulch about 15 minutes from camp. There, King later wrote, "I found upon a tree a water notice, claiming the water right to a small stream." It was signed by Henry Janin, and it wasn't long before they located several similar notices, realizing they were in the midst of the so-called diamond fields.[11]

"Throwing down our bridle reins," wrote Emmons, "we began examining the rock on our hands and knees. In an instant I found a ruby. This was, indeed, the spot."[12]

By dawn the next day, they were all back with magnifying glasses, examining locations of stones and their relationship to natural gravels. Several rubies and diamonds were found on ant hills, but King became suspicious when he discovered a diamond perched on top of a rock, convincing him the mine was salted. He wrote, "The diamond lay directly on top, in a position from which one heavy wind, or a single winter storm must inevitably dislodge it."

They found also emeralds, sapphires, garnets and spinels (spiked rubies) in the same field with diamonds, an impossible conglomeration. They then studied ant hills, discovering that where every precious stone lay, the ant hill had a small hole punched there by a rigid object. No gems were found on untampered hills, strongly indicating the diamond field was a swindle and a hoax.

Now positive there were no diamonds or other gems within hundreds of miles of Ralston City, King slipped out of camp and caught a train for San Francisco, arriving there on November 10.

King arranged an immediate meeting with the directors at Ralston's office and informed them that "the new diamond fields upon which are based such large investments are utterly worthless." He then demonstrated in detail that the diamond field was a huge hoax.

He added that the identity of the swindler did not come within the scope of his investigation.

King was astounded and disgusted when a number of the directors approached him to suggest that he remain silent in public about his discovery, assuring King they would "make it worth his while."

He indignantly refused and threatened that if they did not themselves make it public, then he would.

The public saw King as a hero. The San Francisco *Bulletin* declared in an editorial that the fraud came near to "being one of the most disastrous swindles ever perpetrated."

It is not clear today if Ralston was a victim of the fraud, or its perpetrator. Arnold had been employed by Ralston and Harpending in the Ralston City Burro Mines a couple of years earlier, before the hoax, so Arnold was not a complete stranger to Ralston when they met in the latter's office with the diamonds. Arnold took his share of the $660,000 and went back to Kentucky, where he bought property and started a bank.

It never became clear what role Harpending played in the swindle, but he later wrote a book in an effort to prove he had no knowledge of the fraud.

The town of Ralston rather gradually sank below the surface of the Southwest, to became totally resurrected a few years later, as Shakespeare.

Nobody knows exactly what role William Ralston played in the charade. He became enveloped in eternal silence on the afternoon of August 27, 1875, by wading far out into the Pacific Ocean and never returning.

The townsite eventually became the property of Mr. and Mrs. Frank Hill and their daughter, Janaloo. Mrs. Hill, now deceased, once related a strange event that occurred much later at nearby Lordsburg, which may, or may not, shed some light on this.

"Harpending's son showed up one day at the Chamber of Commerce office in Lordsburg," explained Mrs. Hill. "He told the people there who he was and said he just wanted to look over his father's old haunts, and asked specific directions to certain places, which he was furnished.

"As he prepared to leave the building, the Chamber secretary told him she and other old-timers had often wondered what his father had to do with the affair. She attempted to be pleasant, hoping not to frighten him, and pointed out that all principals were long dead, that the statute of limitations had run out, and all that, concluding with a plea 'that you tell us exactly what part your father played in this interesting old plot'."

Harpending listened politely, according to Mrs. Hill, then

broke out laughing as he walked from the office. He was still laughing when he stepped into his car and drove off.

1. Ralph Emerson Twitchell, *Leading Facts of New Mexico History,* Torch Press, Cedar Rapids, Iowa, 1912, Vol. II, pp. 361-2.

2. Ibid. 367.

3. O. W. Williams, *Pioneer Surveyor, Frontier Lawyer,* Texas Western College Press, 1966, 123-4.

4. Rita and Janaloo Hill, "Alias Shakespeare, the Town Nobody Knew," *New Mexico Historical Review,* July 1967, p. 212, quoting the Tucson *Arizonan,* Aug. 21, 1869.

5. Tucson Weekly Arizonan, Sept. 2, 1870.

6. Ibid.

7. Tucson *Citizen,* Nov. 19, 1870.

8. Thurman Wilkins, *Clarence King,* McMillan Co., N.Y., 1958, p. 159.

9. Ibid. 162.

10. Ibid. 163.

11. Ibid. 164

12. Ibid.

Frank Hill, father of Janaloo, is buried in the Shakespeare cemetery, but the graves are not well kept.

CHAPTER V
Ralston Becomes Shakespeare
(Arky Black Was Too Tough To Die)

Ralston City remained deserted for several years after the diamond hoax. This languid state was gleefully noted in Tucson, where the *Citizen* observed that the place "had become more of a place of note than of importance, a place of many houses but few people, and presents a ghastly appearance compared to what it did in May 1870, when Harpending's gang was cooking up a stupendous swindle in quartz and diamond mining."[1]

Next act in the drama was changing the name of the town to Shakespeare. It was bestowed by a General William G. Boyle, hoping the community would enjoy a dramatic rise in real estate values. Boyle arrived in Ralston City April 10, 1879, according to the Tucson *Star*, and awaited the arrival of one S. M. Ellis to do some survey work on the townsite, recently purchased by the Great Egyptian Khedive, according to Boyle.

Further identification of the Great Khedive was not made public, but it is likely the transaction had something to do with a Dr. James Henry McLean, "Patent Medicine King of St. Louis." McLean, a native of Scotland, was ensconced in lavish offices in the Grand Tower Block in St. Louis, Fifth and Market streets, with laboratories on Chestnut.

McLean appears to have been both a man of science and an advertising genius, claiming to have 85,000 agents traveling throughout the United States, selling his Volcanic Oil Liniment and Little Liver Pills. Dr. McLean was also wealthy, estimating just his floating medical stock at $2 million.

He also was an inventor, having patented a portable military fort and a hundred-shot breechloading rifle, as well as a 100-ton naval gun, with Octopus and Devil Fish torpedoes, which he was then dickering to sell to the Sultan of Turkey.

Despite this, Dr. McLean termed himself a pacifist, having just published a best-seller titled, *UKASE! We Command All Nations to Keep the Peace.*

After purchasing Ralston City, McLean renamed it Shakespeare, incorporated the Shakespeare Gold and Silver Mining and Milling Company, and opened Shakespeare's new post office, naming the durable Johnny Evensen as postmaster.

Dr. McLean's advertising genius soon had out the word that Shakespeare, New Mexico, lay in the very center of an area loaded with gold, silver, diamonds, rubies, sapphires and a lot of other nice stuff, ripe for the picking off the ground.

This message reached Dallas, Texas, early, influencing a recent Harvard Law School graduate and surveyor with a spot of lung trouble he hoped to cure in a dry climate, named Oscar Waldo Williams. He and five other equally impressed young men departed Dallas by stage for New Mexico to try their luck in that state. The group went first to Santa Fe, where they met with the New Mexico Governor, Lew Wallace, who had just finished writing a novel, **Ben Hur.**

The group then filed a number of mining claims that didn't pan out, so they split up, with Williams heading south to inspect the town with the romantic name of Shakespeare.[2]

Knowing nothing of Ralston's recent financial disaster, nor of William Ralston's suicidal walk into the Pacific Ocean, prospectors from all over were attracted to the possibilities and to the fine ring of the Shakespeare name. They flocked in to investigate.[3]

Williams was among them and he grubstaked three others, one named Tom Pettie, another was William Rogers Tettenborn and the third referred to only as Grady. Pettie and Grady went right to work prospecting for pay dirt, but Tettenborn headed for the nearest saloon, where he hoped to find a sociable audience for his stories. He is described as "a tall, gangling man of blond complexion...about 25 years old. His mother was Scotch and his father a subject of the Russian Czar."[4] He would become famous in the territory as Russian Bill.

Working nearby was another trio, led by David Egelston, who had been a Forty-niner to California. With him were Tom Parks and an unusual young man named Robert Black, called Arkansas Black, after his native state, but most often referred to as Arky.

Arkansas "Arky" Black stands in front of his saloon (at right in apron), posing with some of his customers for the photographer.

Arky became a prospector because it afforded him an opportunity to pursue his true calling—that of lover. Arky loved all women, whether short, tall, ugly, beautiful, white, brown, red or black; from north, east, south or west; American, Mexican, African, Indian or Oriental. Arky and Egelston were partners mostly because Dave liked to hear Arky's stories of conquest.

Egelston was a hardworking prospector and knew his business, thus affording Arky time to wander in and out of jacals, haciendas, tepees, and all sorts of adobe dwellings in search of new soul-mates.

They had discovered what they hoped would be a rich strike by September, 1880, in the Gold Hill Mining District, 15 miles northeast of Shakespeare, which they sold promptly to an outfit called Foster & Co.

The partners then split up, with Dave and Parks continuing in their prospecting efforts, but Arky headed back to

Shakespeare, where he was soon famous for being the first to buy a drink, or bet on anything, lend money, laugh at fate, and—of course—continue his love affair with womankind.

It was inevitable Arky would be caught making love to a married woman in a small town like Shakespeare. Getting caught in such a situation is always embarrassing, but not always fatal. Arky had been caught red-handed, or red something-or-other, by an irate husband.[5]

Fortunately, the husband following prudence rather than valor, did not challenge Arky personally, but took his case to a magistrate. The case is not on record, but Shakespeare learned the magistrate ruled in Arky's favor, so the husband took his case to the curbstone. He told a chosen few the juicy details and ended with a warning that Arky might also practice his art upon the partners of other Shakespeare husbands.

A group of family men concluded the thing to do was to get rid of Arky, so a posse of husbands sank two uprights, with a beam between, and produced a rope.

They caught Arky asleep, trussed him up, and held a kangaroo court. To obfuscate the details, Arky was charged with making off with a branded heifer, found guilty, and sentenced to die upon the gallows.

A rope was fitted snugly under his ears and the husbands pulled away at the other end. Arky was hoisted off the ground, legs thrashing, and strange gurgling sounds coming from his throat.

At this sight and sound, certain of his poker-playing and drinking buddies relented. They prevailed upon their companions and Arky was lowered to the ground and given a proposition:

Arky could continue to live if he would leave town and never return.

"Go to hell," Arky shouted in reply. "Hang away. What's the matter? Goin' soft? Hang away!"

Up went Arky into the air again, kicking and dancing on air until his movements became faint, heardly discernible.

Remorse struck again. A spokesman called a halt and Arky once more was lowered to the ground. While he was reviving, sitting on the ground, struggling to get his breath, the spokesman pleaded with him:

"Arky," he pleaded, "please leave town. We don't want to hang you, but you have to leave. This town ain't big enough for a lover as busy as you."

As color flowed back into his cheeks, Arky struggled erect, facing his executors.

"Tellya what," he said. "Give me a couple of six-shooters and I'll whip the whole caboodle of you!"

Roxy Jay, owner of the Roxy Jay Saloon, turned to the postmaster, Johnny Evensen, saying:

"Arky's too good a man to die."

"That he is," replied Johnny.

"I have a suggestion," said Roxy Jay. "Let's make that loud-mouth take his wife and leave, instead of Arky."

As the stage was preparing to pull out of Shakespeare for Tucson that evening, a vigilante group escorted a husband and errant wife to the stage station, bought two tickets to Tucson, placed them aboard and waved their guns in a sentimental farewell.

Not long after this adventure, Arky became a married man himself, but it took a shoot-out to accomplish it, a shoot-out, oddly, that didn't involve Arky. It was over a couple of fried eggs, served up in Shakespeare's only hotel, the Stratford, on Avon Avenue, of course.

This lodging house had been acquired by a flamboyant operator named Fred W. "Beanbelly" Smith, who claimed to be the son of "Extra Billy" Smith, Civil War governor of Old Virginia. He was a guest before he was the owner, and he checked in one night fairly late. He arose the next morning, sauntered into the small dining room and ordered two fried eggs.

The waiter told him there were no eggs, so he ordered oatmeal, which he was eating rather reluctantly when Ross Wood came into the dining room. Wood, a well-to-do owner of the National Mail and Transportation Company franchise, sat down and ordered eggs. He got them. To Beanbelly's chagrin. He arose, walked over to Wood's table, and started an argument over the difference in their treatment.

A shouting match developed and Wood, in a dudgeon, rushed to his room and got his revolver. He returned shooting, as he entered the dining room. Beanbelly fired only once, killing Wood with a single shot.

It is told in awe that Beanbelly sat down and ate Wood's eggs.

After breakfast, he made a deal with the owner to take over the hotel, just to see that it was run properly.

Beanbelly put up with no nonsense in his hotel and business improved to the point he was short of rooms. When Sandy King came to Shakespeare to take up with Russian Bill Tettenborn, Beanbelly was forced to add an additional room to accommodate the pair. He built it onto one side of the adobe structure.

King had recently committed murder, but was free under what was known as "straw bail," or a bond signed by irresponsible individuals.[6]

The Southern Pacific Railway was laying tracks rapidly across the plains and reached a place near Shakespeare called Pyramid Hill. This necessitated the use of a large number of draft horses, and all were branded with a P.I. As they approached Shakespeare, a few began disappearing each night.

Russian Bill boasted one night in Beanbelly's saloon that he and King were stealing them and selling them up north at a good price. This conversation was overheard by an S.P. employee, who could see he would be out of a job if this kept on. The employee broke into the room where Russian Bill and King slept. He roped the self-proclaimed horse thieves and strung them up from the saloon rafters.

With Beanbelly's cooperation, the bodies were left dangling for more than a day, until the next stage arrived, "to serve as a warning to incoming passengers that Shakespeare was a place of law and order," as Beanbelly put it.[7]

Meanwhile, Ross Wood's widow, Jessie, convinced Arky Black he would do well to marry her. She said she could supply the money to buy him a fine new saloon in the new railroad town of Lordsburg, about two miles north of Shakespeare, on the Southern Pacific line.

Arky and his new bride moved to Lordsburg, opened the Silver Dollar saloon, and prospered, catering almost exclusively to railroad workers.

The Silver Dollar gained the reputation of being the best

run saloon in Lordsburg. Arky kept order himself. When he wasn't angry, just cautious, he wore a .45 pistol on his waist. When he expected trouble, or was riled, he carried it in a holster.

Arky's customers trusted him. Whenever they needed his help, he gave it. This was demonstrated when the first railroad strike hit, a strike of telegraphers.

When the first strike-breaker arrived in Lordsburg and began tat-tatting messages from the depot, Arky strapped on his gun and went to the depot to meet the noon train. He walked in on the telegrapher, drew his gun, and told the scab that he must hurry outside, get on the arriving train and never come back.

The telegrapher hesitated, so Arky shoved the .45 in his face.

"Get on that train and leave," he ordered, but about then the train started moving slowly out of the station. Grabbing the telegrapher by the arm, Arky ran down the platform, pointed the gun in the engineer's cabin and warned: "Don't move that train, mister, until I tell you. . . and I ain't going to tell you until this dirty skunk leaves with you!"

When the train didn't stop fast enough to suit him, Arky shouted, "Do as I say, or I'll blow you right out of that cabin!"

The train halted instantly and the strike-breaking telegrapher was placed aboard.

The next day came a warrant for Arky's arrest, charging him with detaining the mail, but Arky was slipped advance notice and he departed for Mexico. Only a couple or three days later, though, he was back at the Silver Dollar.

"I can't stand that damned tequila," he explained.

Arky's wife asked Judge Benjamin Titus what the penalty might be if he turned himself in, suggesting that Arky wanted to know if the judge was prone to a deal.

Judge Titus became so incensed he exploded with some injudicial language to say what he thought of a man who would send his wife on such an errand.

Mrs. Black returned in tears. That was too much for Arky. He buckled on his hog-leg pistol and stalked into Judge Titus's chambers. Arky was about five-foot-six and the judge over six feet, with whiskers. Arky grabbed the judge by the whiskers, pulled his head down and shouted: "You are a black-hearted bastard and no part of a man to make a woman cry."

He hit the judge on the head with the barrel of his pistol, and pistol-whipped the bigger man as he crumpled to the floor. Before Arky could saddle a horse and head for the border once more, he was arrested and thrown in jail, this time getting a year's sentence. Most of his sentence was served, however, in the Las Cruces, N.M. jail. According to the Silver City *Enterprise,* Arky didn't like the accommodations in Las Cruces, so the sheriff turned him over to Deputy George Saylor, who hauled Arky to Silver City to serve out the rest of his time.

What effect the jail term had on Arky's behavior is inestimable, but it gave his wife, Jessie, grounds for divorce, which she obtained while Arky was in the hoosegow. Mrs. Black then married a railroad engineer named Jim Barnett, an old friend of Arky's and one of his best customers at the Silver Dollar. The former Mrs. Black and her new husband moved to Tucson before Arkansas was released from jail.

When he did get out, Arky returned to Lordsburg, married a dance-hall girl, but it didn't last. He was now proprietor of the St. Elmo saloon and installed a new-fangled contraption that had been invented while he had been away—called a cash-register.

Arky not only bought the first one in Lordsburg, he became famous for the way he operated it. Arky was a maestro with money. After each sale Arky would wave his hands around, like a concert pianist, carefully selecting the proper keys, ring with the proper finesse, clink the money into the slot, and bump it closed with his belly. He confessed privately that he bought the cash-register to entertain the customers, not hold money. Once, while demonstrating his virtuosity at the cash keyboard, Arky confided: "I don't trust nobody with my money. I only let them play around with it for a little bit."

Arky never put away enough money to retire, though. He lived it up. When his feet and legs gave out and he couldn't tend bar anymore, he sat down to play poker for a living. When Arky ran out of funds, friends would stake him again, and again, and again. Bartenders kept him in free drinks.

Arkansas and his old friend, Jim Barnett, who married the former Mrs. Black, remained on good terms. Whenever Barnett came to Lordsburg, Arky set up the drinks. After several years, Barnett died, a relatively wealthy man, leaving his entire estate to his widow. When Jessie heard that Arky was not making out too well in Lordsburg, she came over to see him.

Arky was living in a hovel, but was too proud to accept charity from the former Mrs. Black. He did finally agree that if the Barnett widow truly needed him, he would rejoin her. Jessie hauled him over to Felix Jones' barber shop, where he was given a bath, shaved and had his hair cut. He was then hauled over to Robert and Lehay's General Store and fitted out for a new suit.

Many of Arky's fans and friends were on hand at the station when the train pulled out, including the late Mary Dee Kipp and Claude C. Freeman, also a Lordsburg resident, both of whom supplied most of the information for this summation of Arky's career.

Mary Dee said Arkansas winked just as the train pulled out of the station.

Freeman explained, though, that it might have been a cinder.

Or a tear.

1. Tucson *Citizen*, April 13, 1877.
2. O. W. Williams, *Pioneer Surveyor—Frontier Lawyer*, edited and annotated by S. D. Myers, Texas Western College Press, El Paso, 1966, p. 94.
3. Mrs. Emma M. Muir, New Mexico Magazine, XXVI, Nos. 7-8-9-10, 1948.
4. Williams, *Pioneer Surveyor—Frontier Lawyer*, p. 94.
5. Details of sexual encounters are seldom published, so the details of Arky's adventures were related to the author by those who knew Arky and listened to his confessions. One of these was Mary Dee Kipp, daughter of John and Emma Muir, a Lordsburg founding family. Another was Claude Freeman, also of Lordsburg, who knew Arky well and told his story to the author.
6. O. W. Williams, *Pioneer Surveyor*, p. 95.
7. Ibid. fn. pp. 161-2

CHAPTER VI
Billy the Kid Could
(A Frightened Boy—A Notorious Outlaw)

It was mid-afternoon, April 18, 1881. A slight youngster with auburn hair and a pleasant countenance sat in a jail cell at Mesilla, New Mexico, writing a letter on a scrap of paper, addressed to Edgar Caypless, the boy's attorney in Santa Fe. It read:

> *I would have written this before but could get no paper. My United States case was thrown out of court and I was rushed to trial on my Territorial charge. Was convicted of murder in the first degree and am to be hanged on the 13th day of May.*[1]

The attorney to whom he was writing probably would have written it "hung," and so would most of the lawyers of that time and place.

The boy wrote on, apologizing for the cramped writing, and explaining, "I have handcuffs on."

He concluded with, "I remain as ever, yours respectfully," and signed it "W. H. Bonney." Bonney, of course, was Billy the Kid, known in Silver City during his school days there as William Henry McCarty, later as Billy "The Kid" Antrim, the latter name being that of his stepfather.[2]

Billy was requesting the Santa Fe lawyer to retrieve a racing mare stolen from him by law officers at the time of his arrest. He instructed the attorney to sell the animal at auction, so he could obtain money to appeal his death sentence for the murder of Sheriff William Brady of Lincoln County.

Over the years a mythic perception has grown around the character of the so-called Billy the Kid, maligning him with the perception that he was uneducated, devious, homicidal and a liar, plus a number of other unflattering adjectives, except one for which there may be some evidence: that he might have had homosexual tendencies.

He probably was not as bad as most of the characters around him, and he certainly was not unschooled. Fate contrived to send him a teacher better qualified than many in the United States of that day. She was Mary Richards, who arrived in Silver City about the same time as he did. She became his teacher as a result of unusual accidents, including a shipwreck.

In 1857, before Billy was born, a sailing vessel departed Liverpool, England, bound for the United States. On it was Dr. John Edward Richards, a physician; his wife, Mary; their daughter, Mary, aged ten; and two sons—Ruben, 14, and Edward, eight.[3]

During this voyage, the crew mutinied, killed the master, and took over the ship. A fire broke out and the flames nearly went out of control before Dr. Richards succeeded in taking command, putting out the fire, then putting down the mutiny. He managed to bring the vessel into the port of Galveston, TX, where he turned it over to the authorities.

Dr. Richards set up a medical practice in Brownsville, a community less than ten years old. Within a year his wife succumbed to yellow fever and Dr. Richards was murdered by Indians while on a sick call.

The children, as a result, became wards of the British government. A family friend, Lord Salisbury, arranged for the children to be delivered back to England. Meanwhile, the boys were left with a family named Primm, and Mary was placed in a Catholic Mission.

When a British friend of the family arrived later in the United States he had no trouble finding Mary, but couldn't locate the boys. Mary alone was returned to England, where she was placed under the care of a Dr. Bailey, regent of St. Aden's College, South Hampton.

Under Dr. Bailey's guardianship, Mary became one of the best educated young ladies in the British Isles, perhaps in the world, maybe of all time. It would seem impossible to equal, much less better, her credentials. Mary was proficient in German, Spanish and Italian, as well as in English and its literature. To improve her idiom, and perfect her accent, she spent one year in all three foreign countries. Upon her return to England, she became the official translator and interpreter for the Prime Minister of England, Benjamin Disraeli.

Mary was also selected as literary translator for poet Alfred Lord Tennyson, as well as for John Ruskin, art critic and writer. She enjoyed a lifelong friendship with both, cor-

Mary Richards, translator for Prime Minister Benjamin Disraeli, and a friend of John Ruskin, had this picture taken in England shortly before she left that country to search for her lost brothers in Texas. She later became Billy the Kid's teacher at Silver City, New Mexico.

responding regularly with them while living on the Southwest frontier, where she became the school teacher of little Henry Antrim, destined to become the notorious outlaw, Billy the Kid.[4]

Mary arrived in the Southwest in 1873, searching for her brothers, Ruben and Edward, reported to have been adopted and settled in the Southwest. Military authorities at Fort Stockton told her a Don Ricardo Richards held a big meat contract to provide beef and other provisions to that fort.

Mary, however, located him living at Ysleta, Texas, married to the daughter of a wealthy haciendado, Don Felix, who had settled his son-in-law in the business of cattle-ranching. Ruben, meanwhile, had acquired a substantial amount of wealth and a large, Spanish-speaking family. It was he who arranged for Mary's school-teaching job at Silver City, NM.

Mary eventually married a rancher named Casey and they had several children, one of whom was Patience Glennon. Mary and her brothers have many descendents living presently throughout the Southwest, many of whom speak only Spanish. Upon Mary's arrival, Ruben had eight children, four boys and four girls. The girls were Cecilia, Blasita, Maria and Severa, while the boys were Ruben, Jr., Eduardo, Francisco and Ricardo.

When Mary arrived, Ruben was planning to enter the freighting business, which he did, passing on to several generations of his boys a freight line operating until the 1960s.

Ruben informed Mary that their younger brother, Edward, had remained in the Matamoras area, where he had taken up ranching. Both of the boys had served in the Civil War, but on different sides—Ruben with the Union, and Edward in the Confederate cavalry.

After locating her brothers, Mary was still faced with the problem of where she would live and what she would do. She would prefer to live in the United States, she told her brothers, but didn't think she was qualified for any kind of frontier occupation...unless it were to teach school. But where?

Brother Ruben had inlaws living in Silver City and they informed him that city was planning to organize its first

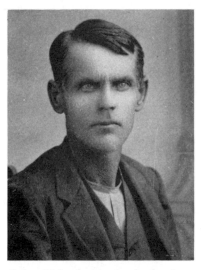 

Ruben Richards, Mary's other brother, was a mining operator. He sired a large Spanish-speaking family.

Edward Richards, Mary's older brother, was a rancher at Ysleta, Texas. Known as "Don Ricardo," he supplied beef to the Union Army.

school. A communication with authorities there confirmed Ruben's assumption and said they would be delighted to have a teacher with Mary's qualifications.

To reach Silver City alive was another question. The road to that village passed through the most treacherous part of Apache country. She took a coach to Mesilla, New Mexico from Ysleta, and in Mesilla boarded one headed into the outlands of the west, with the next terminal Tucson.

They made it without event to Fort Cummings, but there they had to outrace a war-party of Apaches who struck them at Cooke's Pass. They finally arrived with all hands safe, but well frightened, at Uncle Dick Hudson's stop at Hot Springs.

That September, Mary opened the first school in Silver City. From the beginning, she was helped by a pleasant, buck-toothed little fellow, small for his age, who cheerfully performed most of the chores, such as carrying water from the well to fill the drinking container inside the school, sweeping out, and fetching firewood when cold weather set in. He was Henry McCarty, who would become both famous and dead as Billy the Kid before too many more years would pass.

William Henry McCarty looked like this while attending school in Silver City, New Mexico, where he was taught by Mary Richards.

Billy's mother, Catherine, operated a boarding house in Silver City while married to William H. Antrim, a miner who was temporarily following the butcher's trade. Catherine had contracted tuberculosis while living in Wichita, Kansas. After becoming ill, she sent the boys to Indianapolis, Indiana, for a short time to live with relatives until her condition had improved.

It is not clear exactly who the blood father of the two boys was, but it probably was Michael McCarty, of the Fifth Battery, Indiana Light Artillery, who died of wounds at Chickamauga in 1863. His estate, according to government records, was one pair of shoes, a hat, a blouse, pair of pants, a pipe, 50 cents, a battered wallet and a three-cent stamp.

Henry's mother was industrious. She organized a laundry in Wichita and bought a fairly large amount of land in that city, including a quarter-section now the heart of Wichita. Catherine sold that property in 1871, and moved to Denver with her sons, hoping the climate would halt her lung disease.

Catherine went to Santa Fe a short time later for the same reason, and, after marrying Antrim, moved to Silver City, which was booming then as a copper mining district.

This is a portrait of Catherine McCarty, mother of Billy the Kid, before she married William Henry Harrison Antrim.

William Henry Harrison Antrim, step-father of Billy the Kid, in a photograph taken in the 1890s at the portal of a Confidence Mine in New Mexico.

Catherine went back into the business she knew best in Silver City, opening another boarding house and this time her son waited on table, according to one of the boarders, Sigmund Lindauer, who came to the Southwest originally searching for diamonds. When diamonds there proved to be a hoax, Sig's total assets were a Sharp's rifle, which he immediately sold and used the money to visit friends at Clifton, Arizona, who set him up in the mercantile business at Silver City and nearby Georgetown, where a huge stamp mill was being erected.

Millwrights and miners flocked to Silver City from all parts of the United States and Canada, mostly to work in the mills. Among these came an Irish Canadian, Daniel Casey, who wooed and won Mary Richards. After their marriage, the couple had several daughters, one of whom was Patience. She continued to live in Silver City until her death in 1964.

"What mother thought and said about Billy," declared Patience, "is completely different than what other people said about him. It seems to me that whenever I tell what mother knew first-hand about him, there are four or five know-it-alls who never knew him, didn't live in Silver City and most of them weren't even born yet, but they would pop up to contradict her and ridicule me.

"Mother said the only serious trouble she knew Billy to be in was nothing more than a childish prank. When some roomers left a trunk full of clothes in his mother's boarding house, Billy and another boy, George Schafer, known as Sombrero Jack, opened the trunk, dressed in the clothes and paraded up and down Silver City streets dressed as women.

"Silver City had strict laws against this kind of behavior. They were arrested as transvestites and were thrown in jail. Billy was very small, so he managed to crawl up through a chimney and escaped."

Mary Richards and her husband, Casey, had moved to Knight's Ranch, located several miles southwest of Silver City, and Billy walked one whole night on foot without being detected from the jail to the ranch, trying to find a place to hide.

"Mother told me," related Mrs. Glennon, "how he showed up there, frightened, and he told her in great detail what had happened. My mother explained to him that this was not a serious offense as child's play, that the law was meant to control the actions of sexual deviants on public streets. She advised him to head right back to Silver City and give himself up, explaining that the penalty he might receive would be nothing at all compared to the misfortunes which would afflict him if he were to run away."

Patience explained that her mother said Billy headed back on the road to Silver City, but evidently became frightened again while thinking it over. Apparently, he turned off the road—still riding the horse Mary Richards had loaned him—and headed in the direction of Arizona, away from Silver City.

Mary Richards told her daughter, "We didn't hear any more from him until he got into trouble in Arizona. This time it was serious."

Billy had departed Knight's ranch in August 1875, and had then worked on several cattle ranches, after which he became a teamster at Camp Grant. It was there he was dubbed, The

Kid. Besides being small, Billy didn't look to be as old as he was, according to a contemporary, J. W. (Sorghum) Smith, who operated a hay camp in Pima County, Arizona, who said Billy was "a good boy... I never thought The Kid would have turned out that way. He came to my camp at Fort Thomas (on the Gila River, below Solomonville) and asked for work. He said he was seventeen, but he didn't look fourteen."[5]

Billy also worked as a civilian teamster at Camp Grant, just west of the Arizona-New Mexico border. He was employed there by Captain G. C. Smith to drive a logging team from a timber camp on Mt. Graham to a sawmill on the Post. It was here that Billy really did kill a man. The murder took place at a small village, called Bonito, in Adkins' Dance Hall, south of Camp Grant.

Herman Lindauer, the son of Sigmund, also operated a men's clothing store at Deming and he explained that his father talked to him many times about Billy the Kid's escapades. Herman said his father told him that "at Camp Grant there was a blacksmith named Frank P. Cahill, but most people called him Windy. One day Windy called Billy a pimp, and Billy returned the compliment by calling Windy a son-of-a-bitch, at which Windy picked Billy up and literally threw him off the floor of the dance hall."

Herman said an eye-witness later told his father, Sig, "Billy had no choice. He had to go for his equalizer." Billy, then known as Henry Antrim, shot the bigger man and when Cahill died the next day, Billy lit out, away from Arizona.

According to the Lindauers, it was shortly after this that Billy joined up with John Kinney's band of cattle rustlers. Billy then moved on up into northern New Mexico and finally got a job with John Tunstall, to whom he became quite attached. Billy explained why, "He treated me with respect, like a man."

This move placed Billy smack in the middle of what has been called a range war, but was apparently a contest between two groups of so-called businessmen fighting to see which bunch would end up with the very lucrative grazing rights on government land.

Billy applied to Tunstall for a job, perhaps aided by his former teacher, Mary Richards, who was also from England, as was Tunstall, who had come to this country only a short time before.

Opposing the Englishman was Tom Catron, boss of the territory, backed by a staunch lieutenant, Major L. G. Murphy and Jim Dolan, who arrived in New Mexico as a soldier in the California Column during the Civil War.

The Murphy-Dolan men, livestock thieves masquerading as a quasi-military group, were caught stealing Tunstall's horses. Tunstall, Billy's pal and boss, rode out to remonstrate and was shot in the back of the head.

Billy received word of this atrocity the same evening, and was furious. He leaped on his horse and rode to Lawyer McSween's office in Lincoln. Upon arriving, he found a posse already forming to arrest Tunstall's murderers. The Kid joined the posse, which took off immediately.

Two of the gang, Morton and Baker, were chased down almost immediately, but getting them to trial proved impossible. While on the trail, Morton maneuvered his horse beside Deputy McCloskey, grabbed his pistol from its holster, and shot the officer dead. Baker managed to work loose and they fled.

All of Billy's mounts were race horses, so he had little difficulty riding down the two thieves and shooting them to death, legal under the circumstances, since they had killed a deputy and were attempting to escape.

Nevertheless, William Brady, Lincoln County Sheriff and a hireling of the Catron gang, swore out murder warrants for The Kid's arrest. Before they were served, however, Sheriff Brady was killed from ambush, and Billy was also charged with this murder.

Meanwhile, the Lincoln County Range War had grown so bitter the United States Army was drawn into it. The Fort Stanton Commandant ordered out an infantry company and another of artillery to maintain the peace until somebody could be found to volunteer to be sheriff.

After a short stalemate, George W. Pipin, one of Catron's lackies, arranged to take on the job long enough to trap Billy and his followers. This was finally accomplished in McSween's home.

The soldiers set the house on fire, forcing the occupants to

William Henry Bonney, or Billy the Kid, displays all of his artillery while hiding out from the law.

flee, including Billy, who leaped through a window with both guns blazing to make his getaway, along with most of his followers. Lawyer McSween was not so fortunate. He was murdered by the so-called lawmen.

Historian Robert N. Mullen thinks this is the high-handed activity that put a halt to the Lincoln County War.[6] The murder of Tunstall and McSween was too much to pass off as the killing of horse-thieves, resulting in Billy becoming the hero of the common man in the territory. He has remained so since, even though attempts are still made to picture him as "an adenoidal killer."

"Our grasp of the Lincoln County situation will be strengthened," wrote Mullin, "if we remember who and what Henry McCarty, alias Kid Antrim, alias William Bonney, actually was, before circumstances remodeled him into an immortal outlaw."[7]

1. William A. Keleher, *Violence in Lincoln County, 1869-1881,* University of New Mexico Press, Albuquerque, 1957, pp. 320-21.

2. Grant County *Herald,* August 3, 1878, "Kid" Antrim's Real Name is W. H. McCarty. The latter was the name of his blood father.

3. The complete history of the relationship between Billy the Kid and his teacher, Mary Richards, is provided by numerous interviews with Patience Glennon, in 1960. The latter was the daughter of his teacher, Mary Richards. Information from the interviews, held at the home of Mrs. Glennon in Silver City, resulted in a series of articles for the El Paso *Herald-Post.*

4. Author's interview, Patience Glennon.

5. Robert N. Mullin, *The Boyhood of Billy the Kid,* Southwestern Studies, Monograph No. 17, Vol. V, No. 1, Texas Western Press, El Paso, 1967, p. 15.

6. Mullin, interview with author in latter's home, Columbus, NM, 1961.

7. Mullin, *The Boyhood of Billy the Kid*, p. 23.

CHAPTER VII
The Fall Guy
(Mystery Man of the Territory)

Mary and Daniel Casey finally gave up ranching in 1880, and moved to Georgetown, a mining community near Silver City. There they raised a family of three girls and three boys: Blanch, Edith and Patience; John, Samuel and Daniel.

"My mother quit teaching to devote full time to her family," explained Patience Glennon. "The last time she saw Billy was after the burning of McSween's house. She said Billy was in a fit of despondency and had been down on the Mimbres River, visiting his brother, Joe, who was older than Billy. Billy told mother that when they parted, both had tears in their eyes, that they kissed and Joe remarked that would probably be the last time they would see each other alive.

"Billy showed mother his horse, knowing she was a horsewoman, and told her he had gotten his horse from an Apache down on the Mimbres—that he had shot the Indian and took the horse. He also told mother that he desperately needed money. Mother gave him all the cash she had in the house, voluntarily, not from fear, but more in sympathy, realizing his predicament. Billy and mother spent the balance of the day talking.

"Mother told me that, somehow, both knew this would be the last time they would have the opportunity to talk, and that Billy was reluctant to go for this reason. She said they talked for several hours, until well after sundown and it was well into the night before Billy mounted up and took off riding south. She said it was obvious he knew that he didn't have long to live, but was determined to set things right as he saw them.

"My father came home that night all excited. He rushed in and said to mother, 'Do you know that no-account Billy the Kid is on the loose again? He was seen riding toward Georgetown. I wonder what he is up to now?'

"Mother replied, 'Yes, I know. He was here almost all day, but he's gone now and I'm sure he won't be back. I gave him what money I had here, the poor boy!' Mother never told me what my father said to that."

Mrs. Glennon folded her hands in her lap, and added: "People may contradict me, but that is what I personally know about Billy the Kid. That's the way mother told it to me."[1]

Mrs. Glennon's account fits well with the information supplied by the late Herman Lindauer, owner of a men's clothing store in Deming, NM, whose father, Sigmund, was a friend of Billy. Sigmund lived with the Antrims when Billy's mother ran a boarding house in Silver City.

"My father," explained Herman, "lived at the Antrim boarding house for quite a spell and he knew both Billy and Billy's brother, Joe, as well as Catherine and Mr. Antrim. My dad told me the last time he saw Billy was one day when he was riding from his Georgetown store to Silver City. He saw Billy coming along on a horse from the direction of the Mimbres River. Billy was also headed for Georgetown, and he called to my father and asked if the road was clear from there to Georgetown. Dad said he thought so, and Billy rode on in that direction. Dad went on into Silver City. That was the last time they were to meet."[2]

United States census records for 1880 show that Billy the Kid's official residence was in Georgetown on June 10 of that year, for it was then the census taker found Billy, listing him as "occupant 174" of "dwelling 193" and put him down as a "dairyman" whose name was then "William McCarty, age 21."

After his escape from the Lincoln County jail, Billy had been hanging out at various cow and sheep camps, most of which were owned by John Chisum. Some of Billy's old friends were even turning away from him, including his old pal, Pat Garrett, who had come to that part of New Mexico in the fall of 1878. Pat was a native of Louisiana, but had left that state in 1868 as an 18-year-old youth.

Miguel Antonio Otero, at one time a popular governor of New Mexico, knew both Billy and Pat intimately.

"For nearly two years," wrote Governor Otero, "Pat Garrett was a personal friend of Billy the Kid. They were on the most intimate terms, and around Fort Sumner were generally known as Big Casino and Little Casino. The Kid made his headquarters in the Garrett saloon; they drank and gambled together. If Pat won he staked The Kid; when The Kid won he staked Garrett. It was rumored that Pat and The Kid were partners."[3]

Otero explained that Pat, more cunning than The Kid, negotiated with Captain J. C. Lea, Chisum and several other big cattlemen on the Rio Pecos, promising that if they got Garrett elected sheriff, he would "get rid of The Kid." In short, Pat Garrett was two-faced and unprincipled, so it was easy for him to become elected Lincoln County Sheriff on a promise he would break up cattle and horse thievery and do away with his chum, Billy the Kid, by murder if necessary.[4]

Life came to an end for Billy on the night of July 14, 1881, when he rode into Fort Sumner to have his last supper with Jesus Silva. Billy wanted steak, but Jesus didn't have any, suggesting that Billy walk over to Pete Maxwell's nearby home and slice himself off a piece from a yearling calf slaughtered that morning.

Maxwell lived in a huge residence, one originally built to house U.S. Army officers during the Navajo war, and when Billy approached the entrance he noticed two men loitering in the front, both strangers. They were John W. Poe and Thomas K. McKinney, deputies who had just ridden up with Sheriff Garrett from Roswell. The latter had left them only moments before to have a talk with Maxwell, who was in bed in one of the inner rooms.[5]

Garrett seated himself at the foot of Maxwell's bed, remaining in the dark as he asked Pete about the Kid's whereabouts. While they were talking, the Kid entered and asked Pete, "Quien es?" (who is it?). Maxwell whispered to Garrett, "That's the Kid," and Garrett later told Governor Otero: "I pulled my pistol and fired, threw my body to one side and fired again. The Kid fell dead at the first shot. He never spoke."

Otero said Jesus Silva and a Navajo woman, Deluvina, entered the room immediately after the shooting to find Billy dead, with the butcher knife in his hand. He had no pistol.[6]

Billy was buried the next day, July 15, 1881, "dressed in a borrowed white shirt much too large for him, in a coffin of plain wood in the little cemetery at Fort Sumner.[7]

Much later, Pat Garrett would get his, too, in a similar

fashion, when he attempted to match wits with a man who at that moment was driving cattle from Texas to Oklahoma. That man was Albert Bacon Fall, who was then courting his future wife, Emma Morgan, whose father, Simpson H. Morgan, organized and was first president of the Memphis and El Paso Railroad, later known as the Texas Pacific.

Fall married Emma and sold real estate briefly at Clarksville, Texas, then came to the Southwest with his brother-in-law Joseph S. Morgan, stopping first in El Paso, then moving on up to Silver City to try their hand at prospecting. They prospected for several months in the Hanover and Santa Rita copper districts, then moved on to Georgetown in the Mimbres district, finally trying their luck at Kingston without any better luck.[8]

It was at Kingston that Fall met Edward L. Doheny "and perhaps 5,000 other miners and prospectors" who had been attracted there by the discovery of The Bridal Chamber mine, which produced almost pure silver. Also nearby was Hillsboro, a gold camp.

Short of funds, Fall took a job at $10 a week cracking quartz with a hammer. Doheny had a lease on a site north of Kingston which failed to pay, so he quit mining to practice law in Silver City. Later he moved to California, where he brought in that state's first oil gusher to become a multimillionaire.

Before leaving New Mexico, however, Doheny mightily impressed Fall in an encounter with a drunken miner running amuck. The drunk was taking potshots at Doheny with a six-shooter, but during an intermission when the culprit was reloading his weapon, Doheny pulled his .45 and, intentionally aiming low, shot the miner in the leg. These acts so impressed Fall, he ran to congratulate Doheny on his empathy and composure as well as his marksmanship.[9]

It was about this time that Fall met Frank W. Parker, a lawyer from Michigan. Parker would become a deft politician and New Mexico's Territorial Judge, later a State Supreme Court Justice and charged by Fall to be on the side of the New Mexico land barons.

After failing as a prospector, Fall moved to Las Cruces, opening a book and stationery store, run by his wife while

Albert studied law. He was admitted to the bar in 1899, and, being a Democrat, found himself in a territory run by Republicans and led by Colonel Albert Jennings Fountain, a New England Yankee.

Fall's career was thus reversed, bringing about serious contradictions and ambiguity. Even those people who knew him rather well found they had no firm convictions about either his acts or his convictions. Most of these questions remain unanswered. They are:

1) Was Albert Fall a United States Senator from New Mexico who really lived in El Paso, Texas?

2) Was Fall a Democrat who broke up the infamous Republican Santa Fe Ring under Tom Catron, or was he a Republican appointed to be Secretary of Interior in President Warren Harding's cabinet, with Catron's help?

3) Was Fall as rich as Croesus, or poor as Job's turkey?

4) Was Fall a lawyer who defended gunmen who shot people they didn't like, or was Fall a gunman who shot people he didn't like?

5) Was Fall a legal dandy who wore a Prince Albert frocktail coat and carried a cane, or was he a chuck-wagon cook, a cowboy and one of the best bronc busters in the Southwest?

6) Was Fall a swamper working in Mexican Mines, or was he a partner in one of the biggest copper mines in the world?

7) As Secretary of Interior, did Fall's leasing out government oil fields in Wyoming and California insure the U.S. Navy of sufficient fuel at Pearl Harbor in the war with Japan, or did he accept a $100,000 bribe to award the oil leases to his old-time friend, Edward L. Doheny?

8) Was Fall convicted of receiving a $100,000 bribe from Doheny, who—in turn—was found innocent of giving Fall the bribe?

It is difficult to believe the answer to all the above questions is yes, but to get back to the beginning:

After having no luck as a prospector, Fall became a lawyer, even though he was a southern Democrat practicing in a Republican territory, run by Fountain, a New England Yankee.

Initially, the fact that Fall was in a political minority helped his law practice because he defended the interests of small ranchers, most of whom had migrated from the Confederate state of Texas and remained staunch Democrats in a land of Republicans. One of these Democratic ranchers was Oliver Milton Lee, a former Confederate. They formed an alliance to protect one another—with Fall supplying the cunning, and Lee the fighting men.

The first test came when they presented a full Democratic ticket in New Mexico, a Republican state. Fall was the candidate for the Territorial Legislature and he learned before election day the Republicans were so apprehensive they planned to call out the State Militia "to guard" the polls.

Fall interpreted this to mean they expected to intimidate voters, so he sent word for Lee to bring his men and guns also, which he did. Oliver and six of his best rode all night to arrive in Las Cruces early on election day, taking up positions on the roof of Martin Lohman's store.

Soon the militia came marching down the street, some 50 men in uniform and with rifles, under the command of Major W. H. Llewellyn. When they drew up at the election site, Fall stepped into the street, waved his cane and shouted: "Llewellyn! Get the hell out of here with your damned militia, or I will have you killed. You've got just two minutes."

Capt. A. B. Fall, Company H, First Territorial Infantry, Spanish-American War, 1898

Albert Fall, New Mexico Territorial legislator

Llewellyn's militia halted and Fall pointed to the top of Lohman's store, across from the polling place, where Lee and his men stood, rifles cocked.

The major took in the situation immediately and nodded to his captain to dismiss and disperse the militiamen.

Fall and the Democrats won the election. Fall was sent to Santa Fe to represent his district. To assure his good works would be reported properly, Fall established his own newspaper, *The Independent Democrat*, and brought his father, William Fall, to Las Cruces as editor and publisher.

Most formidable of Fall's opposition was a former U.S. marshal and dead shot, Ben Williams. Fall detested Williams, and with sufficient cause, for Fall had received information that Boss Catron, head of the Santa Fe Republican Ring, had promised to pay Williams $10,000 to kill Fall.

The inevitable confrontation occurred about 10 o'clock one night in September 1895, when Fall and his brother-in-law, Joe Morgan, ran into Williams on a Las Cruces street. All three men went for their weapons simultaneously. Morgan was the first to fire. His shot only creased Williams' head and took off a piece of his ear. Fall's slug plowed through Williams' left arm, above the elbow, and entered his body, causing a serious injury.

Williams was the last to fire, and did little or no damage, but his own injuries were so serious that he spent several months in a hospital recovering.

A Dona Ana grand jury convened to hear the evidence. Fall explained he had received a warning that the Santa Fe Ring had placed a $10,000 price on his head and had urged Williams to earn it. Fall was asked by the grand jury foreman if he had any other reason to shoot Williams.

"Yes," Fall replied. "I don't like him."

The grand jury apparently considered this good and sufficient reason, for it found both Fall and his brother-in-law, Joe Morgan, innocent. The jury also indicted Williams for attempted murder, charging the Las Cruces Republican boss, Albert Fountain, with being an accessory after the fact.

Peace did not settle on the community soon, however. Less than two months after this shoot-out, Fall, his brother-in-law Joe, and Oliver Lee's cowboys nearly became involved in still another gun battle. Fall, candidate for the Territorial Legislature on the Democratic Ticket, was worried that the Democrats, a minority, would lose if Republicans turned out in huge numbers at nearby Tularosa, so Fall appointed Lee and his cowboys to examine the ballot box from Tularosa before it was delivered to the election headquarters in Las Cruces.

The cowboy "committee," well-mounted and well-armed, headed off the election courier, opened the box, counted the votes, and found a heavy Republican majority, so they burned the votes, box and all. The ploy didn't work, however, because the election canvassers—all Republicans—ruled unanimously that if the votes had been counted, all Republican candidates would have won easily.

This demonstrated to Fall that the Democratic victories of the future would be few, or none at all, during his natural lifetime. Consequently, he took the only prudent action open to him: Fall became a Republican.

He also converted Oliver Lee and his sharpshooting cowboys, but the Republicans were not exactly overjoyed at this turn of affairs. The suddenness of Fall's switch was caused by the rapidly approaching date for New Mexico to become a state. This meant the State Legislature would soon appoint two U.S. Senators, and Fall wanted desperately to be one of them.

First, though, came the Spanish-American War, and Fall didn't want to miss that either, proposing a plan whereby the war could be won quickly and easily. Fall asked New Mexico Governor Miguel A. Otero to allow him to organize a company of 50 cowboy sharpshooters and ship them to Cuba "to act in an independent capacity."

Governor Otero turned down the plan, but it was picked up by Teddy Roosevelt for his future Rough-Riders.

Otero did appoint Fall a captain of Company H, First New Mexico Territorial regiment of enlistees. The governor then made sure that Company H never got to Cuba.

Fall did go south to train with his company, however, even if he was not allowed to leave the country. His friend, George Curry (later to become governor of New Mexico) rounded up a large number of cowboys from southern New Mexico to serve in Colonel Teddy's famous cavalry that eventually charged on foot up San Juan Hill.

Upon his discharge from the service, Fall managed to work his way into a more favorable position in Republican politics, serving two terms as Attorney General of the Territory and was elected to the Territorial Council in 1903.

Meanwhile, Fall also built a large law practice, most of which was in Texas. He was also named company counsel for Colonel William Cornell Green, the copper baron.

Fall's distinguished legal reputation came mostly as a result of his brilliant defense of Old John Selman for shooting to death John Wesley Hardin. The latter, the most notorious gunman of the day, was writing his memoirs in a downtown El Paso rooming house. Well past midnight, he put down his pen to seek a little relaxation at the nearby Acme Saloon.

There, Hardin shot dice with the bartender, Henry Brown, for drinks. He sent the dice galloping across the bar, set down the cup and spoke his last words: "Four sixes to beat."

Selman had slipped through the swinging doors and walked toward the bar, quietly, while drawing his six-shooter. He aimed at the back of Hardin's head and fired. The bullet came out under Hardin's right eye.

The El Paso *Times* carried a story the next day which was absolutely the reverse of the story told by eye-witnesses.

"The first shot did the work," the *Times* story recorded. "It entered the eye and came out the back of Hardin's head."

Whether Hardin was shot in the eye or in the back of the head was terribly important to Old John Selman: If Hardin was shot in the eye, it meant the victim was facing his nemesis, but he could hardly have been facing Selman if the slug entered the back of his head.

Captain Jeff Milton, a law officer who had been warned that Hardin was also gunning for him, attended the inquest— just to make sure Hardin was dead. Upon entering, Milton saw Selman sitting at the table, sweating profusely, and "wearing a little black hat." Selman was busy receiving congratulations for ridding the community of a dangerous man with a gun.

Upon spying Milton, Selman extended his hand and said, "Shake hands with me, Cap. I've just killed the son-of-a-bitch. Shot him right in the eye."

"I don't mix with a murderer," Milton replied. "You shot that feller right in the back of the head. You can't shake hands with me, that's certain."[10]

Owen P. White, an eye-witness to many early day events in El Paso, missed witnessing the actual murder by only a matter of minutes. White, employed by the Hixon Jewelry Store, was busy polishing silverware late that night of August 18, 1895.

"It was between ten-thirty and eleven when I neared the Acme Saloon and saw Uncle John Selman sitting on a beer keg, rolling a cigarette," wrote White years later in his autobiography.

"When I was about a block away I heard a shot and looked back. Uncle John was no longer on the beer keg, so I ran to the Acme to see who he had killed this time. I opened the door and there stood Uncle John with his gun in his hand. On the floor about fifteen feet from him with a neat bullet hole right in the middle of the back of his head lay John Wesley Hardin."[11]

White, an early chronicler of El Paso events, relates the highly successful defense subsequently made by Albert Fall when summoned from Las Cruces to represent Selman:

"They tried John for murder and the newcomer from New Mexico, Albert Bacon Fall, stepped squarely into the center of the arena. If he was going to acquit his client he certainly had his work cut out for him.

"The bullet that killed John Wesley Hardin (my father was the physician who conducted the inquest) had entered squarely in the back of his head. John Wesley was standing at the bar shaking dice when Selman pushed open the saloon door and shot him from behind. Those were the undisputed facts in the case. What was this Mr. Fall going to do about it? He showed us.

"Still wearing his long-tailed coat and with plenty of bushy hair sticking straight out in all directions, he addressed the jury. He was eloquent; he was magisterial; he was wonderful. In language that soughed and sighed he rehearsed all the details of the killing, including many that were new to all of us. He made members of the jury see everything exactly the way he wanted them to see it.

"They saw Hardin at the bar shaking dice. They saw the innocent Selman push open the swinging door and enter the saloon; simultaneously they saw the villainous Hardin raise his head and glance into the mirror in front of him. They saw the hand of the

*Albert Fall (left) with Eugene Manlove Rhodes, western author
and a close friend.*

great killer flash to his gun-butt and then they saw John Selman fire. Aided by his powerful nouns, adjectives and verbs, they saw all these things and thus a cold-blooded assassination turned into a clear case of self-defense.

"But that wasn't enough for Mr. Fall. In order to assure a verdict for his client, he thought he had to go a bit further. He did. In an eloquent closing speech he dealt at length on the public undesirability of the deceased gunman. He argued magnificently that El Paso, instead of trying Selman for bumping Hardin off, should tender Selman a vote of thanks and present him with a medal.

"This last statement was a mistake. The jury promptly acquitted Selman and would have done so anyhow. The jurors knew, without having Mr. Fall tell them, that Hardin dead was worth more than Hardin alive. If he had only omitted that part of the address, Mannen Clements, cousin of the deceased, would not have left the courtroom swearing that someday he was going to get Albert Fall."

Mannen Clements was destined to make more than one attempt to carry out this threat, too, but was fooled each time, the last one fatally.

1. Patience Glennon, interview with author in Ocotober 1960, at home of her daughter, Mary Bulware, Silver City, NM.

2. Herman Lindauer, interview with author in Deming, NM, October 1960.

3. Miguel Antonio Otero, *The Real Billy the Kid, with New Light on the Lincoln County War*, Rufus Rockwell Wilson, Inc., New York, 1936, p. 92.

4. William A. Keleher, *The Fabulous Frontier,* University of New Mexico Press, 1962, p. 73.

5. Otero, *The Real Billy the Kid*, p. 188.

6. Ibid, p. 190.

7. Keleher, *Fabulous Frontier*, p. 73

8. *Memoirs of Albert B. Fall*, edited by David H. Stratton, Monograph 15, Southwest Studies, Texas Western College, Vol. IV, No. 3, 1966, p. 24.

9. Ibid.

10. J. Evatts Haley, "Jeff Milton a Good Man with a Gun," U. of Oklahoma Press, Norman, 1948, p. 248.

11. Owen P. White, *The Autobiography of a Durable Sinner*, G. P. Putnam's Sons, New York, 1942, p. 57.

CHAPTER VIII
Adventures of Flipper
(First Black Graduate of West Point)

Henry Ossian Flipper, a mulatto who became the first black cadet to graduate from West Point, was born at Thomasville, Georgia, March 21, 1856. His mother, Isabella, was the property of a Methodist preacher, Reuben Lucky. His father was Festus Flipper, a shoemaker owned by E. G. Ponder.

The preacher decided to retire in 1859 and move to Atlanta, taking his slaves with him. Festus, who had saved sufficient money working on shares with his owner, bought his wife, Isabella, and his son, Henry, from the departing preacher, then "loaned" them to his owner, Ponder.[1]

Henry explained in his autobiography that of the 65 slaves owned by Ponder, nearly all were mechanics, permitted to "hire their own time... were virtually free. They acquired and accumulated wealth, lived happily and needed but two things to make them like other humans, absolute freedom and education."[2]

Henry's education began when he was eight, with a private tutor. In 1866, he transferred to the American Missionary Association school, and three years later enrolled in Atlanta University, where, as a freshman, he was appointed to the U.S. Military Academy.

In his autobiography, Flipper said he "was treated by all persons with the Academy as it becomes one gentleman to treat another. I refer to servants, enlisted men and employees. They have done for me whatever I wished, as I wished, and always kindly and willingly, to the exclusion of others. This is important when it is remembered the employees, with one exception, are white."[3]

Flipper expressed a thought before its time in another place, declaring "Equal rights will come in time. Moreover I don't want equal rights, but identical rights. The whites and blacks may have equal rights and yet be estranged from each other."

Flipper also scoffed at the idea equal rights were denied

because of skin color.

"It may be color in some cases," he wrote, "but in the great majority it is mental and moral condition."

Lieutenant Flipper graduated from West Point on June 14, 1877, and turned down an offer to become Commander in Chief of the Army of the newly created country in West Africa, Liberia. "I have no sympathy whatever for the 'Liberian Exodus' movement."[4] This was the plan to ship all blacks in the United States back to Africa, setting them up in their own country. Flipper was happy he had been removed from Africa when his ancestors were shipped to America as slaves.

Two black cavalry regiments, the Ninth and Tenth, were formed by an act of Congress in 1866, and Flipper was made Post Signal Officer to instruct Tenth Cavalry enlisted men on the basics of military signalling at Fort Sill. Flipper's captain was Nicholas Nolan, a 50-year-old widower with two small children, who departed shortly after Flipper arrived for San Antonio, where he married Miss Annie Dwyer, some 30 years younger than Nolan. He brought back both his new bride and her younger sister, Mollie.[5]

"Mrs. Nolan insisted that I should board with them," Flipper wrote in his *Memoirs,* "so I discharged my cook and did so. Miss Dwyer and I became fast friends and used to go horseback riding together."

Flipper's immediate superior, First Lieutenant R. J. Pratt, joined the company at Fort Sill and in the spring of 1880 Flipper's troop and two others were ordered from Sill to Fort Davis, Texas, a 1200-mile march. Upon arrival at Davis, they were transferred to Fort Quitman, on the banks of the Rio Grande.

Their first taste of fire was in a battle at Eagle Springs, where three men were killed and buried where they fell. Flipper was detailed to read the Episcopal service over them, after which a volley was fired and taps sounded. As a reward for services in the field, Flipper was made Acting Post Quartermaster and Acting Commissary of Subsistence," meaning he was in charge of the military reservation, including houses, water, and fuel supply, plus transportation, feed, clothing and equipment.[6]

Essentially, Flipper was in financial control of Fort Davis and after a spell of malarial typhoid, he was able to mount a horse again and assume full duties. It also meant he and Miss Dwyer might take long rides again. But not for long.[7] A new First Lieutenant from the ranks of the Civil War Army was sent to Fort Davis as Flipper's immediate superior. He was Charles E. Nordstrom, described by Flipper as "a Swede who had no education and was a brute."

Flipper wrote, "Nordstrom hated me and gradually won Miss Dwyer from her horseback rides with me, and himself took her riding in a buggy."

A second blow came when Colonel W. R. Shafter was transferred from the all-white First Infantry to become commanding officer at Fort Davis.

"He at once relieved me as Quartermaster," wrote Flipper, "and informed me he would relieve me as Commissary as soon as he could find an officer for that place."[8]

A court martial was then convened at Fort Davis on November 4, 1881, with Colonel Galusha Pennypacker, 16th Infantry, presiding, with two charges lodged against Flipper: the first, "Embezzlement of $3,791.77" and, second, "Conduct unbecoming an officer."

Lieutenant Flipper pleaded not guilty, testifying that the shortage was due to other officers, for which he was found not guilty. He was, however, found guilty "on four specifications" of conduct unbecoming an officer and was dismissed from the service until charges were appealed to the President of the United States Chester A. Arthur, who confirmed the sentence.

Flipper then sold his three horses and other privately-owned property to various civilians, and departed for El Paso, where he remained until the fall of 1883, at which time he was employed to survey certain lands in Mexico.

Ft. Davis, Texas, looked like this at the time of Lt. Flipper's court martial on charges of embezzlement. Court proceedings took place in the building at left of flag staff.

A Mexican company was formed to survey its public lands and these rights were transferred to an American company which engaged A. Q. Wingo, who knew of Flipper's capabilities and he hired Henry as his assistant.

Flipper and Wingo finished surveying the line between the states of Chihuahua and Coahuila on Christmas Day, 1883, and returned to Meogqui, a railroad town about 50 miles south of Chihuahua City, where they rented a house and began preparing their maps. A couple of days later, the Mexican police arrested Flipper, "throwing him into a filthy Mexican jail." Even though he spoke excellent Spanish, Flipper could not make out what his crime was. Fortunately, General Carlos Pacheco, governor of Chihuahua, was a big stockholder in the Mexican company for which Flipper's outfit was working, so he was released without learning why he was arrested.[9]

Henry learned later it resulted from a letter he had written to a Negro friend, George Ashbridge, an El Paso barber, in which he observed that in Mexico "women do not lose their caste when they lose their virtue...the priest in Santa Cruz is living openly in adultery and he and his 'girl' are received everywhere."

Flipper's friend gave the letter to S. H. Newman, editor and owner of the El Paso *Lone Star*, who published it February 9, 1884, and on February 14, Flipper was in court charged with slander against a priest, Cura D. Manuel Terrazas, a member of one of the richest and most powerful of Mexican families.

Flipper was quick to retract all such slander and explained his was a private letter to a friend, anyway, and a few months later he was even offered a commission as "colonel in the Mexican Army at a handsome salary."[10]

He was also offered and turned down a full professorship at the Military Academy of Mexico at Chapultepec. Flipper declined, he said, because it was necessary to become a Mexican citizen in order to get it."[11]

A short while later Flipper did accept employment by the city of Nogales, Arizona, to prepare its land grant case for the Court of Private Claims, performing such a thorough and accurate job that the citizens of Nogales tendered him a banquet, an honor which ultimately got him into active politics.

One Nogales doctor refused to attend the banquet, giving as his reason that he would not eat at the same table as a Negro. A few months later, the same doctor ran against another Democrat for school trustee, and Flipper worked hard for the doctor's opponent, who won the primary and was ultimately elected by the voters.

Flipper also became involved later in a political battle of greater importance. Chairman of the Nogales Republican Party was a man named Altschul, who made up a list of delegates to the Arizona constitutional convention, with his name at the top. At the suggestion of Jesse Grant, son of General U. S. Grant, Flipper and he made up their own slate and beat Altschul "just for the fun of it." They had slates made, with Altschul's name deleted, and the latter was soundly beaten, becoming "so chagrined" he sold his property in Nogales and went to Teguciggalpo in Honduras, "where he went to raising sugar."[12]

Republicans were so impressed with Flipper's political savvy, he was made a temporary editor of the Nogales *Sunday Herald* newspaper, while the regular editor attended the Territorial Legislature. The session lasted four months, during which, said Flipper, he "had great fun," He was then appointed special agent for the Department of Justice and served in that capacity until July 1901, when he was employed to gather information to defeat James Peralta Reavis in his attempt to steal about half of the state of Arizona by calling himself The Baron of Arizona. Flipper gathered and translated various documents in both this country and in Spain exposing the Baron as a fraud.

At the outbreak of the Spanish-American War, Flipper offered his services, but his telegrams were ignored, so he accepted the post of resident engineer for the Balvanera Mining Company, at Ocampo, Mex. The Balvanera Company headquarters was in New York, with William G. McAdoo its president and an internal battle over who should be general manager finally caused it to become inoperative. The company was sold in 1905 to Colonel William C. Greene, Cananea Copper King, and Greene's first assistant, Albert Fall. They asked that Flipper remain as engineer, and he agreed.

The company engaged in no mining activity while the company worked at raising cash, a situation which turned Flipper's duties into becoming host to and entertaining parties of rich capitalists who visited there to look over the property. During one of Colonel Greene's trips to Ocampo, Flipper told him about the lost Taypoa mine, and Greene dispatched Flipper to Spain, where he studied old maps, records, and archives to learn where it was, but nothing came of it.

Treasure hunters still are rooting around that part of Mexico, searching for secret doors which might lead to tons and tons of ancient gold and silver. Someday, maybe.

Col. William C. Greene (the big man at left) greets a few of his friends at the railroad stop as they arrive for his huge feast, prepared by his partner Henry Flipper, late of the U.S. Army.

1. Henry Ossian Flipper, *The Colored Cadet at West Point, an autobiography*. Homer Lee & Co., New York, 1878, pp. 7-8.

2. Ibid. pp. 8-9.

3. Ibid. p. 161.

4. Ibid. p. 272.

5. Henry O. Flipper, *Negro Frontiersman, the Western Memoirs of Henry O. Flipper*, edited, with introduction by Theodore D. Harris, Texas Western College Press, El Paso, 1963, p. 2.

6. Ibid. pp. 17-18.

7. Ibid. p. 19.

8. Ibid. p. 20.

9. Flipper, *Western Memoirs*, p. 26.

10. *Lone Star*, May 6, 1885.

11. Flipper, *Western Memoirs*, p. 48.

12. Flipper, *Western Memoirs*, p. 32.

CHAPTER IX
Fall and Greene Join Up
(Nobody Knows Where the Bodies Are Buried)

Mystery attracts attention and the disappearance of the Fountains was a real who-done-it. Colonel Albert Fountain, a New Yorker, attended Columbia University, then went on a world tour which ended in Hong Kong where he and others were imprisoned for being aboard an opium-smuggling craft. After the American consul got him free, Fountain went to San Francisco, studied law and was admitted to the bar. He enlisted in the Union Army at the outbreak of the Civil War, became a captain of cavalry and was wounded in a skirmish with Apaches in Arizona.

Sent to El Paso for treatment, Fountain recovered and was made a customs house officer at the Port of El Paso, but quit to organize the artillery for the army of Benito Juarez, who made him a colonel. In 1868, Fountain was elected to the Texas State Senate by obtaining 139 votes where there were only 122 eligible voters in that district.

In 1875, he returned to practice law at Mesilla, N.M., and as a Colonel in the First Regiment of the New Mexico Cavalry he helped chase Chief Victorio and later Geronimo. He was appointed special counsel under Grover Cleveland to prosecute federal land frauds and in 1888 became speaker of the New Mexico House from Dona Ana and Lincoln Counties.

On January 31, 1896, Albert Fountain and his nine-year-old son, Henry, were traveling in a buckboard enroute home from a term of court in Lincoln County when they disappeared so completely that it became a nationwide sensation. Two years later Oliver Lee and Jim Gililland were charged with their murder and they went on trial at Hillsboro, New Mexico, before Judge Frank Parker for the murder of Fountain and his young son.

The national press was on hand and there was even a story going around that Sherlock Holmes might come over from London. To insure up-to-the-minute results worldwide, Western Union built a telegraph line from Hillsboro to Lake

Valley, where it tied in to the Santa Fe railroad telegraph facilities.

Reporters were on hand from all the El Paso papers and from many major dailies and wire services throughout the country. The press, typically, began its coverage long before the trial started, with Publisher John H. McCutcheon of the El Paso *Graphic* haled into court by Judge Frank Parker several days before the trial opened and placed under a $500 bond for contempt because the court didn't like the way *Graphic* stories were being worded. Judge Parker informed McCutcheon the bond would be returned when he "worded his dispatches with greater discretion."

Hillsboro was, and still is, a beautiful little mining town nestled away in Percha Valley, its main street proliferated with huge shade trees. In those days Hillsboro had a brick court house, a large Union Hotel and Bar, a number of smaller hotels and enough bars to accommodate only a small portion of the huge crowd which flocked in from all over the world.

The town was 20 miles from the closest stop on the Santa Fe, at a place called Nutt, next to Lake Valley. This was served by the Lake Valley, Hillsboro and Kingston Stage and Express Line, owned and operated by Sadie Orchard, a British born madam, who was equally proud of her whore houses. Her husband was titular owner of these businesses, but everybody knew Sadie was the real boss, 100-percent.[1]

Witnesses for Thomas B. Catron, special prosecutor, were put up in tents at the north end of town, complete with their own cooks, waiters, guards and entertainment. Oliver Lee's defense camp was set up at the south end of town, complete with a chuck wagon for all visitors.

Area mines suspended work so employees could come to town for what appeared to be a number of holidays.

Oliver Lee was the star of the show. The popular rancher had friends all over the Territory and many had come to show their support, with the cowboys, miners and cattlemen fairly certain Lee would never be convicted, and in case he were found guilty, they had plans to take care of that.

Three cowboys were picked to occupy the same seats every day nearest the windows and they listened carefully to the testimony because it had been agreed that if Oliver was convicted, they would hold up the court with their six-shooters and escape out of one of the windows with Oliver. Fast and sturdy horses were saddled, bridled and ready to go at all times. Oliver was to be placed aboard one of these mounts and race for the Mexican border a few miles south. Relays of other mounts were stashed every three miles or so to guarantee his reaching the Mexican border.

Albert Fall, Oliver's lawyer, was sure his client would go free, however, because of a Latin word he knew called *corpus-delicti*, meaning they would have to produce a body before they could claim anybody was murdered.

The state's case was, indeed, weak. Witnesses could say only that they saw Fountain and his son riding a buckboard here or there and that wagon tracks indicated the vehicle turned off the road between Tularosa and Las Cruces. Tracks of three horses were seen, according to State's witnesses, and some spent cartridges were found on the ground. A number of bloody coins lay nearby in a pool of blood. Some horse hairs might have been from one of Oliver Lee's mounts.

That was it. No bodies produced, nor was there any other evidence available to prove that either or both of the Fountains were dead.

Chief witness for the prosecution was from an Albuquerque doctor who confirmed the blood contained in a certain chunk of soil was human, and that some horse hairs belonged to one of Lee's mounts.

When Albert Fall finished with this physician, he finally admitted he didn't know what he was talking about.

The defense produced evidence there were lots of people who didn't like Colonel Fountain, one describing how he had pulled off the biggest election fraud in history, the time he got more votes than were registered voters.

The most they presented against Gililland was that he had uttered an unfriendly statement about Fountain.

There were 18 days of testimony in all and when it closed, the plan was for Harvey Ferguson and Harry Dougherty, associates of Fall, to make the closing arguments, but Oliver Lee insisted that Fall do it personally.

Fall agreed and stepped forward to make an argument

Hon. A. B. Fall

unprecedented in the history of the Territory.

"Gentlemen of the jury," Fall began in a low-pitched voice, "the prosecution of Oliver Lee is the result of a conspiracy to send an innocent man to the gallows."

Fall's voice rose as he continued with, "The district attorney is involved in that conspiracy; the Honorable Thomas B. Catron is involved in that conspiracy..."

Here Falls' voice roared as he turned and pointed directly at Judge Parker.

"His honor on the bench is involved in that conspiracy!"

Judge Parker's gavel was banging before he could reach his feet.

"Mr. Fall," he shrieked, "unless you withdraw your remarks about this court from the jury immediately, I shall send you to jail for contempt!"

Fall drew erect. In a quiet voice he declared:

"Your honor will not send me to jail for contempt until I am through addressing the jury. When I have finished my argument, you may do whatever you wish."[2]

Parker did not carry out his threat, mostly because it would have been taken by Lee's cowboys as evidence of an unfair trial. Shooting would have started and an attempt would be made to spirit the defendants out of the courthouse and send them on their way to Mexico.

The jury was out for only a few minutes.

"Not Guilty," said the foreman.

Outside the courtroom, Fall told his friends his fee was $62.25.

"That's the money I actually spent," he explained. "I took most of my meals at your chuck wagon during the trial."

This gesture was long remembered by his friends, but was not really a great sacrifice. Albert Fall's legal practice and business activities had produced a superb living.

Long associated with Mexican mining projects, Fall's experience in this field had been well rewarded by Colonel William Cornell Greene, who had started out with a butcher shop in Tombstone and turned it into a mining, lumber and railroad empire.

At first, Greene had employed Fall as his chief counsel, but Albert had since advanced to something approaching a full partnership, largely because of his fluent Spanish, knowledge of mining and his consummate political skill on both sides of the border.

When Greene bought the Balvanera Mining Company, he made Fall vice president, as well as second in command of such others as the Greene-Cananea Copper Company, the Sierra Madre Land and Lumber Company, the Rio Grande, Sierra Madre and Pacific Railroad, as well as co-owner in a railroad Greene was then constructing which ran from Greene's mines in Cananea, stretching across northern Mexico to the East into Juarez.

Greene was at that moment planning to build a bridge across the Rio Grande from Juarez to El Paso, so he could connect his Mexican railroad with a major carrier on the United States side, perhaps the Southern Pacific.

Fall, chief counsel for this project, soon hit on a novel way to expedite the endeavor, or at least make money in the attempt.

The era of electrically powered street transportation was seen as the latest and most modern form of getting city folks from one end of town to the other, even in New York.

In El Paso, Mayor Richard Caples administration had

William C. Greene, age 35

issued a trolley-car franchise to a group led by Zach White, Joseph Magoffin and Anson Mills, El Paso's top business men. But even they were finding it difficult to raise money for their new fangled project, so in 1901 they turned their franchise over to a Boston company, Stone and Webster.

El Paso electric trolleys made their first run on January 11, 1902, starting from the center of the city, called Pioneer Plaza, and running a few blocks north and south and over the present bridge to Juarez.

A new train depot was completed on San Francisco Street and El Pasoans expected Stone and Webster to build one of the trolley lines to that magnificent institution. But Stone and Webster refused, declaring there wasn't enough business to make it financially interesting. Owen P. White, who recorded much of early El Paso's history, relates how all but one of the town's citizens were satisfied with the new mode of transportation, except for its not running to the depot. But not Albert Fall.

He complained that in the business part of town the tracks ran down the middle of the streets and when they reached the end of the block, rectangles were formed and became seas of mud every time it rained, so large flat stones were laid to keep pedestrians' feet dry—to the hack drivers' chagrin. There were no storm sewers, so intersections became mud in summer, but when winter rains rushed down Oregon Street and Mesa, the business section of town turned into a lake.[3]

Charlie Davis was elected mayor in April 1905, on a platform to do something about this. The council wanted to know how imperative electric power companies were in other places, so they visited them to find out. To placate Fall, who had helped many of them get elected, they presented him with a franchise empowering him to parallel every street car line in the city.

Fall's partner, Greene, had acres and carloads of ties and rails sitting in Juarez after Greene's railroad was finished in Mexico, so Fall asked if he might borrow them for a few days.

He hired a huge gang of men who moved them, overnight, across the river and stretched rows of ties and rails throughout the downtown, lying parallel to the Stone and Webster track. Traffic was stopped totally and remained so until Stone and Webster saw fit to talk with Albert Fall.

After this discussion, the rails and ties were picked up and shipped to their destination in Mexico, with Fall confiding to White that this little deal netted him $30,000.[4]

With this additional $30,000, plus what he had saved from a lucrative law practice and his association with Greene, he had amassed enough capital to purchase what appeared to be his undoing: the Three Rivers Ranch, a property destined to become many thousands of acres of trouble for Fall. Its name was Tres Rios in Spanish, but to Fall it was heaven.

He took title to the lush ranch property on January 26, 1906, purchasing it from an early settler, Pat Coghlan, who came over from County Cork in 1845. After serving in the U.S. Army, Pat bought the ranch in 1852 to insure sufficient range to produce a constant supply of beef cattle to fulfill a contract he had signed with Fort Stanton to supply it with beef.

Whenever cattle became short, Coghlan is said to have hired Billy the Kid to take his gang over to the Texas Panhandle and steal some, but after Billy was shot to death in

1881, Pat was forced to rustle on his own when supplies got low. Charlie Siringo arrested him once for having hides with the wrong brands, but Pat managed to beat the rap in court, but the legal fees were so high and he was getting so old, he decided to sell.

Coghlan had signed notes at banks for large loans, paying 12 and 13 percent per annum, and was hard-pressed, so Fall bought the two largest notes at a reduced price, paid Coghlan a negotiated amount for the balance, and thus obtained a warranty deed for another 50,000 improved acres, including orchards, groves and some very fertile land.

Soon Fall had nearly doubled his investment by instituting improvements literally unheard of in that day, especially in the Southwest, for which he went deeply in debt.

Nearby Sierra Blanca mountains were crowned with snow almost all year, insuring streams of sparkling water cascading down upon the ranch in sufficient quantities to run a hydro-electric plant, supplying electricity to the whole layout after he built one for $50,000. His wife Emma planted trees, flowers and shrubs in huge quantities. She also bought property of her own. About a month after Fall bought Three Rivers, she bought four lots in the 1700 block of Arizona Avenue in El Paso, in a development known as Golden Hill Terrace.

She then built a huge mansion on them, a structure that still stands in elegant glory. It contains six large bedrooms, each with a fireplace and mantel, on the second floor. The ground floor boasts a music room, a drawing room, a huge library and a dining room, all with polished oak parquet floors.

The house was finished in 1907 and was occupied by the Falls when they were not at their Three Rivers Ranch. Albert maintained a legal residence in New Mexico also so he could hold state offices there.

Two more unsolved murders involved Fall at about this time, also, albeit peripherally: the shooting to death of Manny Clements and Pat Garrett.

Clements threatened to "get" Fall since the day the latter suggested John Selman should be awarded a medal for killing Clements' cousin, John Wesley Hardin, and he tried several times. Once Mannen pulled a gun on Albert in the Coney

Island saloon, but he didn't shoot because there were too many witnesses. One year later, in the same saloon, Clements got full of hootch and announced he was going to kill Fall. He pulled a gun, but was over-powered by three bystanders who threw Clements out of the saloon.

Clements' third such trip to the Coney Island was his last. He was served a drink, then threw his head back to toss it off and dropped dead with a bullet to his throat. No witness could be found who would say what happened, but a meeting was held the following day at the Fall mansion, at which time instructions were issued to the prosecuting attorney, sheriff and constables that nobody was to be arrested or tried for the killing.

The police chief was not invited, so he arrested the bartender on charges of shooting Clements, but the bartender went free because nobody could be found to testify they saw him do it.

Mark Thompson, prosecuting attorney at the time of the killing, confided to Owen White many years later how the shooting might have happened.

Thompson, who quit as prosecutor to become Albert Fall's law partner, said that while Clements was tossing off a drink, the bartender could have been polishing glasses with a large white cloth, big enough for a six-shooter to have been hidden in, and that after a large explosion the gun was dropped into the soapy water.

That *might* have happened, said Thompson, but nobody will ever know.

Pat Garrett was killed February 28, 1908, while driving a horse and buggy between Tularosa and Las Cruces, with Carl Adamson riding beside him. They passed J. P. Miller—a cousin of John Wesley Hardin—on the road, and later they came upon Wayne Brazel riding a horse toward Las Cruces. Garrett got into an argument with Brazel over some goats on Garrett's pasture and, according to Brazel, Garrett reached for his shotgun. Brazel was forced to shoot Garrett in self-defense.

Adamson corroborated Brazel's story, and Albert Fall defended him in court. Brazel was acquitted by a jury within 15 minutes after they left the jury box.

The prosecuting attorney, of course, was Mark S. Thompson.

1. *The Southwesterner*, Vol. 1, No. 6, Jan. 1962, Columbus, N.M.
2. Keleher, *Fabulous Frontier*, pp. 270-77.
3. Owen P. White, *Out of the Desert,* McMath Co., El Paso, 1923, pp. 228-9.
4. Ibid.

Emma Fall and daughters Caroline (sitting on arm of chair), Alexina (standing), and Jouett, taken about 1905.

CHAPTER X
Holmdahl, Soldier of Misfortune
(Emil Built His Own Army)

Emil Holmdahl, soldier of fortune and misfortune, was born of Swedish parents at Fort Dodge, Iowa, in 1883, one of eight children. Emil's older brother, Monty, joined the U.S. Army at the outbreak of the Spanish-American War in 1898. Emil also tried to enlist at the same time, but was turned down because he was too young, so he went to Kansas City, hired a man to act as his father and give parental permission and the hoax worked.[1]

Emil was approaching 80 when interviewed at his daughter's home in Van Nuys, California, but he was still erect, lean, tough, strong of voice and energetic. He was also preparing for another trip to Mexico, where he held a huge land-grant in Baja California from the Mexican government—provided he was able to colonize it within a prescribed time. He was also still drawing pay as a colonel in the Mexican army.[2]

In June of 1962, Emil was busy preparing to depart once more for Mexico, where he was attempting to colonize his huge land grant with refugees from Algeria, people of non-Islamic background who did not choose to become residents of France nor remain citizens of Algeria when that country was given its independence.

Discussing his early days in the U.S. Army, Holmdahl said he was discharged from the U.S. Army in 1906 in the Philippines, and sailed for San Francisco, arriving there just one day before the great earthquake. Emil was knocked out of his hotel bed and that building collapsed around him, but he was not seriously injured.

Some four square miles of the city was demolished and restoration demanded a huge labor force. Emil, who had worked for his father in the building trade, was skilled in carpentry, pipe-fitting and electrical wiring, so he was soon putting in 12-hour days at good wages. In about a year he had saved a lot of money and took a job with the Southern Pacific Railroad, then preparing to lay track south to Mazatlan and east across Mexico. They needed a man with military skills to guard payroll money wagons. Emil rounded up a force of about 250 men for his brigade, many with Spanish-American War experience.

Southern Pacific agents were fanning out ahead to negotiate with landowners for the purchase of right-of-ways. Because Mexican currency was unstable, most sellers demanded payment in gold, so Holmdahl's job was to protect several wagons loaded with gold traversing a country that had more bandits than soldiers.

Emil had learned to speak Spanish in the Philippines and experience there had also taught him that with primitive people the only sure deterrent to stealth was death. There were initial attempts to pillage the wagons, but Emil and his sharpshooters killed every single participant and left the bodies to rot on the desert floor. The attacks became fewer and feebler, then none.

Emil Holmdahl, the famous soldier of fortune who rode with Villa but didn't cut off his head.

After Holmdahl thought he had his job under control, his unit's camp was infiltrated one night by a large band of peons who made off with several hundred horses. The theft was not discovered until dawn, after which Emil mounted a search party, which returned to report the invading force was large and headed due east at a slow pace over rising ground, so Emil divided his men into four parts. The first he sent around the slow-traveling horse thieves to get in front of them. The second and third units he dispatched north and south of the thieves' line of march, with instructions to advance at the same rate of speed as the enemy.

Emil took charge of the fourth troop personally and concentrated it at the enemy's rear, effectively throwing a loop around the whole bunch of peons. He slowly tightened the loop as they advanced, until the peons, realizing they were surrounded, chose to surrender. Not a single life was lost and all the horses were recaptured.

Holmdahl had the leaders of the horse thieves brought to him.

"I asked them why they tried to steal our horses," Emil related, "and they told me they were starting a revolution, that they eventually hoped to join with Madero, who was seeking to overthrow the brutal dictator, Porfirio Diaz."[3]

The more Holmdahl talked with his captives, the more he sympathized with their cause. He also saw a juicy role for himself—that of military leader with a just cause.

"They needed me, and I needed them," explained Emil, "but they needed me more because I was a professional soldier. They were just some guys out to get killed unless they found a military leader with experience—that was me."

Since the right-of-way negotiations were virtually completed, Emil resigned his job guarding the gold wagons. He placed his assistant in charge and selected some key men to join him in the new venture, then he took off with the rag-tag band to help overthrow Diaz.

As part of his settlement with Southern Pacific, Emil obtained a couple hundred head of horses, then took off to realize his dream of commanding his own army in a little war. Emil's men were equipped at his expense, and he began teaching them how to fight. His brigade was soon well-armed, well mounted, and ready.

Holmdahl opened his campaign in western Mexico, where it was easy, picking off a small number of weak government units, then preparing to lay siege to Mazatlan, but then word arrived that Dictator Diaz had already capitulated, gone into exile, first in Cuba and then in France.

Squabbling broke out among the revolutionary leaders seeking to challenge Madero for the top spot. Pascual Orozco, backed by the powerful Terrazas family, was favored because they held virtually the whole state of rich Chihuahua.

Pancho Villa, only a captain in the battle of Juarez, had become a major leader there and elsewhere in northern Mexico, so he moved rapidly into the Madero hierarchy, moving up to colonel, then general, but Pancho had no interest at all in politics. When Madero was elected president, Villa resigned from the army and went back to stealing cattle to supply his butcher shops.

Madero had been in office only a few months before Pancho received an invitation to visit with him in Mexico City. There, Madero confided to Pancho that he had received word that Orozco was plotting with Albert Terrazas and Juan Creel—both old Diaz supporters—to instigate an uprising against Madero in Chihuahua state.

"Go back to Chihuahua," instructed Madero, "and watch Orozco. Keep me informed."[4]

Villa was soon to report that Orozco had made himself "King of Chihuahua." Madero instructed Villa to recruit a strong force to oppose Orozco, assuring him of arms and money. Within days, Orozco attacked the Chihuahua State Penitentiary, but was repulsed. Villa was at his home only a few blocks away from this action when the firing broke out.

By mid-morning two companies of Orozco's men showed up at Villa's home, telling him the attack had failed and Orozco had disappeared, leaving the men on their own.

"My Colonel," said their leader Faustino Borunda to Villa, "we cannot find General Orozco. He ordered us to take the Penitentiary, but we couldn't. Will you take command?"

Villa at that time did not completely trust Borunda, suspecting some sort of trick, so he conferred with Chihuahua Governor Abraham Gonzalez, who gave Villa permission to raise his own troops.[5]

Pancho then left Chihuahua City for the rural areas and within a few days had enlisted an army of 500 men. When word of the recruiting spread, Pascual Orozco, Sr., father of the general, tried to bribe Villa into retiring to private life, but failed.

Madero appointed Villa a brigadier general, placed him under the direct command of Victoriano Huerta, and together they defeated Orozco, with the help of forces under Emilio Madero, brother of the president.

Then Villa became ill with the flu and was taking sweat baths and alcohol rubs to overcome its effects at a time Huerta demanded that he come immediately to Huerta's headquarters. Pancho sent back word that he was indisposed, but Huerta insisted, so Pancho—still with a high temperature—arrived at Huerta's headquarters the next day at sunrise, wrapped in a blanket.

Villa was then made a prisoner and condemned to be shot for insubordination.

Pancho was stood before a wall, preparatory to being executed, but he threw himself to the ground, groveling and "pretending to beg, but only fighting for time," he said later in his *Memoirs.*"[6]

Fortunately, Raul Madero telephoned his brother, the president, in Mexico City, telling him of the situation and the president countermanded the order, ordering Huerta to send Villa to Mexico City, where he was placed in a comfortable prison, taught to read and write, and then allowed to escape.

Pancho then came north by boat, docking at Mazatlan where Holmdahl's force was gathered, but Emil was not informed of his arrival, mostly because Villa was disguised and was traveling under the name of Jesus Jose Martinez.

With Pancho on this trip was a young law clerk from Mexico City, Carlos Jauregui. Together they went by train to the outskirts of Nogales, Sonora, stepped off the slow-moving train and walked across the international boundary into Nogales, Arizona. There they caught a train for Tucson, where they remained four days before continuing on to El Paso. Upon arriving there, Villa notified Chihuahua Governor Gonzalez of his whereabouts and the latter sent him 1,500 pesos. Pancho borrowed an additional 3,000 pesos from his brother, Hipolito, and returned to Tucson, where Sonora Governor Jose Maria Maytorena gave him an additional 1,000 pesos. With these funds, Villa bought guns, ammunition and saddles, but had only enough money left for six horses.

Pancho Villa and his favorite horse,
Siete Leguas

Then Madero was assassinated in a coup d'etat by General Huerta, who proclaimed himself president.

Villa needed three more horses desperately, so he sent three of his men to an El Paso livery stable on three successive days to rent horses and return them promptly, paying each time, to build confidence, so that on the planned day of departure the liveryman would not be suspicious. Then they rented horses and crossed the border with them into Mexico in early April 1913, at La Partidos, west of El Paso.

They entered Mexico in the late afternoon and rode all night to have breakfast at Ojo de Samalayuca. One week later they arrived at San Andres, home of Villa's future wife, Luz Corral, sister of one of his early supporters, Leonides Corral.

Other anti-Huerta leaders went on the attack also, with Colonel Alvaro Obregon chasing Huertistas out of Naco and

Nogales, while the new governor of Coahuila, Venustiano Carranza, issued his Plan of Guadalupe, a proposal for joining together all anti-Huerta groups and their chieftains into a unified government, with Carranza First Chief. This was accepted.

Emiliano Zapata, strongest leader in the south, however, refused to align himself and this was a cause for future trouble.

All of the other Madero loyalists met at La Ascencion, Chihuahua, to form a united opposition to Huerta. When the message went out, Holmdahl headed east with his entire army for the meeting, arriving in La Ascencion among the first.

"A meeting was called for all leaders to meet at an abandoned grocery store located at the edge of the town," Holmdahl explained. "I was present when it was decided that the officer with the most seniority under Madero would automatically take over command. It happened that Villa's commission was seven days older than that of Maclovio Herrera, so Villa was given command.[7]

"Our first big battle was at San Andres, which we won and captured enough money and stores to put us on our feet." It was in this battle that Holmdahl's personal daring carried the day for Villa's command, a fact officially recognized by the Mexican government in 1952 by an act of the Mexican Congress. Holmdahl captured two cannons from the enemy in this action, the first the Villa forces ever possessed.

"We silenced their whole battery," Holmdahl explained in the later interview, "allowing the balance of his force to over-run the position and take their artillery."

By Villa's own testimony, that launched Villa's command, although he attributed the act to a man "of English ancestry, a certain Hondall, or Jontal," as he was to write later in his *Memoirs*.[8]

It became increasingly obvious to Holmdahl that Villa was not interested in a political solution and for that reason Emil threw in with General Obregon, at about the time Villa challenged the latter and Carranza's regime in two bloody battles at Celaya. These defeats effectively destroyed Pancho's authority, reducing him to little more than a colorful bandit. Villa attempted to regain some status by establishing a port-

Pancho Villa (third from right) and his staff of "hombres" as they appeared when first joining Madero in the 1910 Mexican Revolution.

of-entry at Nogales, but President Woodrow Wilson, recognizing Carranza's growing strength, gave the latter defacto recognition and allowed Carranza troops to be sent by rail across western United States, on American railroads, to strike Villa from the rear at Douglas, Arizona, across from Nogales.

Thus thwarted, Villa attempted to recoup by striking at Hermosillo, to the south, and was defeated there also. Desertions and lack of supplies forced Villa to gather up the remnants of his once-powerful army and limp back into the Sierra Madre Mountains to recover from these defeats and rebuild his once powerful military force.

This proved virtually impossible because it is an age-old tradition to leave losers and join winners in revolutions, and this most of them did.

1. Emil Holmdahl, interview with author at home of Holmdahl's daughter in Van Nuys, California, June 1962.

2. Emil explained that he held the rank of colonel initially in the Madero Revolution, resigned in 1917 to join the U.S. Army in World War I, and in 1952 the Mexican government re-activated his commission as a sort of honorarium. He was not on active duty.

3. Holmdahl interview, 1962.

4. Guzman, *Memoirs of Pancho Villa*, translated by Virginia H. Taylor, U. of Texas Press, Austin, 1965, pp. 53-54.

5. Ibid. p. 55.

6. Ibid. p. 74.

7. Holmdahl interview with author, published in *The Southwesterner*, Vol. 2, No. 4, October 1962, pp. 13-14-18.

8. Villa's *Memoirs*, Guzman, p. 100.

CHAPTER XI
Ah—Sweet Euthanasia!
(The Strange Ending of Ambrose Bierce)

Journalists and wars go together, like apostles and epistles. If you have one, you get the other.

Since the days of ancient Egypt, words have been written on *papyrus*, now called *paper*. One epistle begets another, or a *new* paper. A collection of these become newspapers.

Writers for newspapers usually believe they are divinely inspired, perhaps because they are vowed to poverty, and at the very least possess *jus divinum*, the Roman way of saying *divine right*, and liken their work often to a holy crusade.

Their most popular role, however, is that of war correspondent. It is exciting and often produces fame, with minor riches. If these writers arrive late—that is after the fighting is over—they call themselves *historians*. This comes from the Greek, *historia*, or learning from inquiry rather than from direct observation.

Newspaper writers have been around for a long time, perhaps as long as the Apostles, and at least since 1910, for that is the year they flocked to the southern border of the United States to practice their act during what is called The Mexican Revolution. One of these was John Reed, who wrote about such adventures in a book, ***Insurgent Mexico***. He then went on to Russia in 1918, and wrote ***Ten Days that Shook the World***, a prophetic title to his account of the Bolshevik Revolution.

Those correspondents who went to the Mexican border spent much of their time in the lobby, or bar, of the old Sheldon Hotel in El Paso. Among these newsmen were the best journalists of that era, writers like Lincoln Steffens, the famous muckraker; Floyd Gibbons, of the Chicago ***Tribune***; Sherman Martin, New York ***Sun***; George F. Weeks, New York ***Herald***; and the cartoonist, Bud Fisher, who drew "Mutt and Jeff," and Tim Turner, of the El Paso ***Herald***. Tim knew them all and wrote a book of their escapades.[1]

Some of these correspondents were not famous before coming to the border, but would become so a short time later when they covered World War One.

The oldest of these scriveners was a white-haired veteran of the Civil War, Ambrose Gwinnett Bierce, who had worked toward the Twentieth Century by writing of the Civil War, poetry, short stories, anti-social tracts, novels, magazines, articles and books, all the while employed by various newspapers, including the San Francisco *Examiner*, then owned by William Randolph Hearst. Bierce wrote a popular column titled "Prattle," for the latter, but retired in his sixties. At the age of 72, Bierce went to El Paso, Texas, where he crossed the Rio Grande and obtained press credentials to cover Pancho Villa's army, the most powerful in northern Mexico.

Lt. Ambrose Bierce,
circa 1864

Webster's *New Biographical Dictionary* echoes the theme that Bierce then disappeared into Mexico and his fate is unknown.[2]

Bierce's fate, however, is not "unknown." Evidence is now available to piece together what he did and how he did it. That

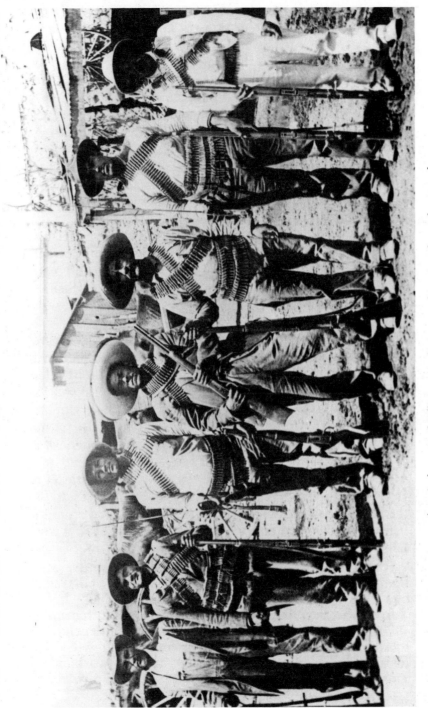

A typical group of Villistas stop long enough to pose for a photograph.

he was beginning to feel his age was made apparent in a letter to B. J. S. Cahill, dated January 20, 1913, in which he admitted: "My work is finished, and so am I."[3]

Paul Fatout, in his biography, *Ambrose Bierce, The Devil's Lexicographer*, presents strong evidence that Bierce went down into Mexico and joined Villa with the intent to end his life in a blaze of action, that "in war-torn Mexico" he would put himself in the way of meeting a welcome death. As he wrote to his niece (Lora Bierce): "If you hear of my being stood up against a Mexican stone wall and shot to rags, please know that I think this is a pretty good way to depart this life. It beats old age, disease and falling down the cellar stairs. To be a Gringo in Mexico! Ha, that is euthanasia!"[4]

Bierce then took a train to Ojinaga, where Villa had collected his troops for an assault against that border city, which he captured after ten days of fierce fighting and many casualties, then he dropped down to Torreon, which he captured to make himself sole ruler of Chihuahua, one of the richest states.

Bierce spent several months, perhaps a year, with Villa and his troops, making himself a favorite mealtime companion of Villa and his staff. Ambrose entertained them with endless stories of his adventures in the Civil War, as well as recounting his adventures in journalism, plus his bright and often humorous anecdotes about life as he saw it. Bierce not only became a favorite of all those who knew him, but devised brilliant entertainment in a dreary situation.

Then came two defeats at Celaya, and a later disaster at Leon, which placed Villa in straitened circumstances, to say the least. After that, Ambrose Bierce disappeared from the face of the earth and nobody could be found who knew what happened to him.

It was not until 1973, more than a half-century after Bierce's death, that Sheila M. Ohlendorf translated the memoirs of Elias L. Torres, a close associate of Villa.[5] It was Torres who negotiated Villa's surrender and retirement in 1920 under excellent terms for the latter, giving Pancho title to a huge hacienda, Canutillo, plus accoutrements with which to run it, plus funds and provisions for his two hundred *Dorados*, the military bodyguards who took up residence there with him.

Torres had been editor of the *El Paso del Norte* newspaper before leaving that job early in the revolution to become Villa's financial agent and advisor, thus he knew Pancho better than did anybody else. Torres tells in his memories how Bierce entertained Villa and his staff at almost every evening meal.

"Bierce spoke very good Spanish," Torres explained, telling how Ambrose was the most popular figure at the table, entertaining Villa and his generals with thrilling stories and funny jokes, "some of which made the famous revolutionary roar with laughter."

Torres also explained that Bierce's hilarious performances were well rewarded financially.

"Villa rewarded Bierce's sallies with munificence," wrote Torres. There were more than a few drafts on New York banks which turned the humorist's jokes into dollars."[6]

Torres continued, "Villa's star began to wane ,when the adventurers who had previously served so well began to change sides...The North American newspapers substituted their eulogies for diatribes and changed their praise to epithets of 'bandit and assassin!' "

Among those who disappeared following the defeats at Celaya and Leon was Ambrose Bierce, who was not seen for several days. When he finally made an appearance, his attitude had changed. He was solemn, not funny at all.

Pancho inquired why he was so glum, and Bierce replied it was because Villa's actions adhered neither to reason nor justice, that his army had become a band of thieves and assassins who did not respect anybody or anything.

At first, Villa took this sudden change in attitude as a prelude to a new joke, Villa and his companions moved forward, leaning closer to Bierce so they could hear the funny twist they all expected.

There was no twist. Nothing funny. Only silence.

Villa arose from the dinner table and General Faustino Borunda (whose son would much later become governor of Chihuahua state) drew his revolver. When he dropped it in Bierce's direction, Pancho grabbed the gun and lowered the general's hand.

Ambrose G. Bierce, 1909

Pancho turned to Bierce, smiled and urged the old man to continue.

"Tell us," urged Pancho, "all the news."

Bierce was silent for a moment, then said the latest news he was aware of came from a very close source: himself.

"I have decided," he said with a broad smile, "to join up with Carranza."

After a moment of awed silence, Bierce explained that Carranza had just been recognized as the official leader of Mexico by the United States, and added that he planned in the future to travel with Villa's bitter enemy, Carranza, saying he had only stopped by for a moment with his mozo (manservant) and horses to bid Villa and his old friends goodbye.

"And now," said Bierce, turning and smiling at Villa and his staff, "I plan to leave immediately."

Villa listened to his farewell with a smile throughout.

Ambrose Bierce as he appeared while accompanying Pancho Villa in Mexico during 1915 and 1916. (Photo courtesy The Ambrose Bierce Papers, M080, Department of Special Collections and University Archives, Stanford University Libraries.)

"That's well thought out, Mr. Bierce," Villa replied pleasantly. "I never hold anyone back by force." Villa opened wide his arms and stepped toward Ambrose.

"Give this old bandit an abrazo and may it please God that Carranza receives you better than I."

Villa gave Bierce a bear hug, almost breaking the small man in two, then the American journalist turned to see if his mozo had their horses prepared for departure. At this moment Villa nodded to Borunda, who left the dining room to follow Bierce at some distance.

While Villa continued his meal, Bierce could be heard speaking to his servant, giving explicit instructions as they mounted just outside the door.

A fusillade rang out from both of Borunda's guns, just outside the door.

"That Gringo," said Villa, turning to his other generals, "has told his last joke."[7]

Bierce, however, may have had the last laugh. Evidence indicates that the acerbic Bierce committed suicide by wit, goading Villa and his officers to shoot him.

Bierce may have been mad, but nobody ever called him stupid.

1. Timothy Turner, *Bullets, Bottles and Gardenias*, Southwest Press, Dallas, TX, pp. 93, 165, 176, 204, 225, 232.

2. *Webster's New Biographical Dictionary*, Merriam-Webster, Inc., Springfield, MA, 1983, p. 108.

3. Paul Fatout, *Ambrose Bierce, the Devil's Lexicographer*, U. of Oklahoma Press, Norman, 1951, fn. p. 312.

4. Ibid., p. 314.

5. Elias L. Torres, *Vibrantes Episodias de la Vida de Villa,* translated by Sheila M. Ohlendorf under the English title, *Twenty Episodes in the Life of Pancho Villa*, published by Encino Press, Austin, TX, 1973.

6. Ibid., p. 36.

7. Ibid., p. 37.

CHAPTER XII
Is It Pork...Or People?
(Sometimes, Light Meat Isn't Appetizing)

Revolutions are not always successful, but they are always expensive. That's why Pancho Villa hired Roy Martin as his border fiscal agent.

Martin, born in Clint, Texas, in 1884, was orphaned as a child and sent to Chicago to be reared by an aunt. She sent him to St. Patrick's and St. Aloysius' academies, and in the summer he worked in a bank and for General Electric, before returning to El Paso in 1909, where he was employed as foreman of the Mexican National Railroad. In this job, he met Raul Madero, brother of Francisco Madero, revolutionary leader and president of Mexico, and subsequently became friendly with Villa.

Dave Wallace, later to become president of Chrysler Motor Co., and Harry Gillis, who would head up U.S. Steel, were operating mines in Chihuahua and had employed Villa to guard their inbound supply trains and outbound bullion shipments from bandits, as did the larger Phelps-Dodge Company. Through Villa, Martin became acquainted with Wallace and Gillis, later joining them in United States manufacturing ventures.

Martin maintained a low profile throughout his life. Consequently, he is almost never mentioned in so-called biographies, history books or articles published in El Paso or Texas, but he was written up in *Who's Who In America,* and was the subject of numerous articles in such publications as *Time, Fortune, Newsweek, Forbes, Barron's* and the New York *Times.*

Martin was undoubtedly the wealthiest man to come out of El Paso, and probably one of the richest even in the state of Texas. During just the year of 1952, the last period for which figures are available before his death, Martin's various businesses netted him $9.8 million, according to his federal income tax statement, the last one filed before his death. Even so, his name appeared in the El Paso *Times* only once during his lifetime and twice in the El Paso *Herald-Post*, according to the El Paso Public Library newspaper index, which also listed numerous articles about him in *Time, Newsweek, Forbes, Barron's* and the New York *Times*, indicating a jealousy on the part of his home-town citizens, or stupid negligence on the part of the publications in El Paso.

Neither is there a single printed source in El Paso press archives telling of his having been fiscal agent for Villa's Army of the North, even though he surely made a lot of El Pasoans rich. Martin placed a single order with the El Paso Hyman Krupp Company for 40,000 khaki uniforms, and a like number of pairs of boots, leggings and coats, which was a huge order for that time and place.

Royce G. Martin, Villa's fiscal agent, who took over the gambling in Juarez following the revolution and made enough money to found Auto-Lite and become a major stockholder in Chrysler Motors.

It was also Martin's job to raise the money to pay for such army supplies, and this job could be fraught with peril. At least it cost him the loss of his right index finger tip, according to a *Time* magazine story about his encounter with a mean individual who owned and operated a Juarez gambling establishment and did not care to ante up his share of the cost of the Revolution.

Instead, the recalcitrant pulled a .45-Colt to demonstrate his displeasure. In attempting to disarm him, Roy accidentally poked his finger into the barrel of the gun. Roy got the revolver from his opponent, but lost his finger tip.[1]

Fiscal agent is how Martin described his job with Villa, but the term is vague. A reporter for the New York *Times* once asked Roy "if he was picked by Villa because of his training or talent as an auditor or accountant." Royce, as he now called himself, looked at the *Times* reporter "as if he had called him a rattlesnake."

"I've been a mechanic all my life," he declared. "I was a mechanic when I served Villa. He didn't know whether a cartridge should cost $7 or $700. I did, and I was able to see that funds were not dissipated, but I was never a bookkeeper."

Late in the revolution, Villa and Martin became apprehensive at the approach of General Huerta's strong forces to the north. They feared it threatened Dona Luz de Villa and Pancho's small family in Chihuahua City, so Dona Luz gathered up the children—a son Agustino and a girl, Micaela—and departed by train from El Paso to New Orleans, where they embarked for Havana, Cuba, on Christmas Day, 1915. She departed with only enough money for hotel accommodations and steamship tickets.

Pancho's brother, Hipolito, remained behind long enough to sell family jewelry for about $30,000, but the broker with whom he was dealing called the police and the jewelry was confiscated, with Hipolito landing in jail. Martin put up a cash bond of $5,000, a trial was held, and it was proved the jewels were not stolen. Hipolito then continued to Havana with his own daughter, Maria Luisa.[2]

Then came "the Santa Ysabel massacre," and Pancho Villa's career went into an almost total eclipse, although it is evident he had nothing to do with it, that it was an aberrational stunt pulled off by Pablo Lopez, a top officer under Villa without the latter's knowledge. It happened on January 10, 1916, at the Chihuahua village, Santa Ysabel, Chihuahua, although the circumstances allowing it began almost a week before, when Charles Watson, general manager of the Cusihuirachic Mining Company arrived in El Paso from Chicago with orders from his board of directors to open the Cusi mines in Chihuahua, which had been idled by the revolution.

Watson and his group departed El Paso on Sunday, January 9, and arrived that evening in Chihuahua City, where they spent the night. At 11 o'clock the next morning, they boarded a Mexico-Northwestern train and arrived at a water stop near Santa Ysabel at about one o'clock in the afternoon. The water tank lay in a sort of valley and soon "many Mexicans appeared on both heights on both sides, armed with rifles. One man covered the engineer and another the fireman. The conductor stepped out to see what was wrong, and was promptly covered."[3]

General Lopez, one of Villa's top officers, told the conductor it was a hold-up and demanded the payroll. They then searched, robbed and killed all of the American passengers except one, who escaped by playing dead, but 19 were killed. Nothing appeared in U.S. newspapers until Thursday, January 14, and this news was transmitted by the British consul in Chihuahua City to an El Paso newspaper.[4]

This delayed coverage so embarrassed the Associated Press that it dispatched its Los Angeles Bureau Chief, George L. Seese, to the Mexican border. Seese spoke fluent Spanish and had covered the early days of the Mexican Revolution, so Villa sent a messenger to Seese, telling him that Pancho had nothing to do with the raid or murders. Seese made preliminary arrangements to accompany Villa to Washington for a conference with President Woodrow Wilson, "in the company of and under the protection of Mr. Seese."[5]

Villa's representative was given a letter from Seese outlining the plan on February 18, 1916, and it was approved by Pancho, who sent word he would be happy to accompany Seese to Washington. But this was not to be, for on March 2, Melville Stone, AP director, quashed the arrangements, notifying Seese not to participate.[6]

Villa, disappointed at losing an opportunity to clear his name, turned to settling some old scores by shooting to death a pair of his oldest companions for betraying him. They were Tomas Urbina and Tomas Ornelas, the former for disobeying orders and the latter for surrendering Juarez, Villa's last port of entry, to his arch-enemy, General Carranza.

Pancho then tried to pull his forces together for a last-ditch effort to challenge Carranza's growing authority over northern Mexico. About 50 of his old marauders showed up immediately, but before long he had 500 men, one band of

Bill McGaw (right) and Dona Luz Corral de Villa, widow of Pancho Villa, in her garden patio in Chihuahua City, where Villa built her a fine home. (Photo taken 1960)

which ransacked the home of Ed Wright, an American who was farming, ranching and working in a saw-mill at Pearson, Chihuahua, to support a wife and three-year-old boy.

The bandits killed Wright and a hired hand, stole their horses and took as a prisoner Ed's wife, Maude. Her maiden name was Hawk until she eloped five years earlier with Ed from Mule Creek, N.M., against her father's wishes. They fled to El Paso, where they were married, then rode on down to Mexico. A neighboring Mexican family at Pearson cared for their infant when Maude was forced to ride off with the Lopez bandidos.[7]

Maude rode for nine days and nights with the Villistas, zig-zagging northward toward the border, during which time Villa told Maude and his men that "If I could stand the hardship, I was to go with his army until we reached the border and there I was to be released," she said. "Villa instructed them that I was not to be harmed and was to eat when they ate, drink when they drank, and if I was unable to continue, I was to be left to die," she related in a 1960 interview.

Hipolito Villa (left) in front of his Chihuahua City home with author Bill McGaw in 1960.

"Once we went three days without eating and many of the men would fall behind. You'd see some soldiers go back to the rear and in a little bit they would come trotting up with the stragglers' horses, saddles empty. I guess they killed them.

"We began riding west, toward Sonora, then headed east, then west again, zig-zagging like Pancho was killing time and was planning to reach the border at a pre-arranged time. There were a lot of stragglers, so Villa would ride up and down the line, smacking them on the back with the broadside of his sword to keep them going. On the way north, they raided Los Ojitos ranch and captured an American Negro cowboy named Buck Spencer. The next day they came upon a Diamond A's round-up and captured three of the cowboys working there." She heard them say they hanged two of them with barbed wire and tied the other one to the ground, then ran over him with their horses, trampling him to death.

"Food was scarce and we seldom had meat, but that night they had meat and I watched them broil it on the ends of their swords," she explained. She said they offered her some of it, but that she refused.

"I thought about them killing those American cowboys like they were butchering cattle and—maybe it was only my imagination—but I couldn't eat the meat. I have remembered all my life that it wasn't red like beef, but was more like pork; it was real light. I went to bed hungry and have been thankful ever since that I did."[8]

She said she had read a lot of Mexican history, including how the Aztec forefathers of these men had routinely eaten each other as their main source of protein.

1. *Time*, March 16, 1953, pp. 100-101.
2. Dona Luz Corral de Villa, interview with author, Chihuahua City, 1961.
3. Ernest Otto Schuster, *Pancho Villa's Shadow*, Exposition Press, 1947, New York, p. 200.
4. Clarence C. Clendenen, *The United States and Pancho Villa*, Cornell University Press, Ithaca, N.Y., 1961, p. 225.
5. Col. Frank Tompkins, *Chasing Villa,* Military Service Publishing Co., Harrisburg, Pa., 1934, p. 41.
6. Ibid.
7. Mrs. Maud Medders (Wright), interview, May 1960, Columbus, N.M.
8. Ibid.

CHAPTER XIII
A Raid Is A Raid Is A Raid
(But Death Can Trade Sides)

The whinny of a horse awakened Lieutenant John P. Lucas at Camp Furlong in Columbus, N.M., shortly after 4 o'clock the morning of Thursday, March 9, 1916. Hoofs crunching on cinders along a nearby railroad bed drew his attention next, then muffled voices speaking Spanish. Peering into the dawn darkness, Lucas made out the figures of horsemen wearing peaked sombreros.

Villistas! The lieutenant leaped from bed in his nightclothes and grabbed his revolver, then backed slowly toward the center of the room, spreading his bare feet into a semi-crouch, facing the door.[1]

Private Fred Griffin, meanwhile, paced guard duty at regimental headquarters. When he spied the horses and heard conversations in Spanish, Private Griffin fired a shot in the air, an act which probably saved the life of Lt. Lucas, but cost the sentry his own; a fusillade of Mauser bullets slammed Private Griffin against the headquarters building, killing him instantly.[2]

Lucas ran barefoot to the barracks housing his machine-gun troop, ordering the first sergeant to turn out the men and follow him to the guard tent, where the machine-guns were kept under lock. There, Lucas found the body of J. D. Yarborough lying across the entrance, felled by another bullet, and he moved it gently to one side, then obtained a Benet-Mercier machinegun, setting it up at the nearby intersection of the railroad tracks and Deming Highway.

After getting off a few rounds, the gun jammed, but soon his men came up with three more and they were put into action. The first gun was then reactivated and within minutes all four guns were spewing death at the Villistas.[3]

While Lucas mounted this defense, Lieutenant James P. Castleman, officer of the day, was alerting F. Troop, where he found that Sergeant Michael Fody had already formed his men. Taking command, Castleman trotted the men to regimental headquarters and ran into a barrage. They didn't answer immediately because Castleman thought it might be coming from U.S. troops, but when he heard them speaking Spanish, the fire was returned. This placed Castleman's 17 men stretched across the northeast corner of the business district and forming a diagonal across the intersection of Boundary and Broadway streets.

The Commercial Hotel, at the west end of Broadway, had by now been surrounded by a hundred or so Villistas under Colonel Cervantes. They were chanting "Viva Villa! Viva Mexico!" and firing into the two-story frame building at random. Jolly Garner, a U.S. Customs Inspector (whose brother, John Nance Garner, would become vice-president under President Franklin Delano Roosevelt) stripped blankets and sheets from beds on the second floor of the hotel, twisted them into a rope, and attached one end to a water pipe. Jolly dangled the other end out of a rear window and lowered the hotel manager's wife and two daughters to the ground, where they were met by Juan Favela. Juan hid them in his residence behind the hotel, until it, too, went up in flames.

The Main Street of Columbus prior to the raid. Covered wagons (at left, rear) were a common sight in those days.

Villistas, meanwhile, broke down the front door of the hotel and rushed in to search for loot. Almost immediately they encountered Uncle Steve Birchfield, a local rancher, at the top of the second floor stairs. Cannily, Uncle Steve tossed

Many Columbus residents picked up their belongings and headed for the mountains after the raid to avoid the possibility of an encore.

all of his pocket money on the floor below and on the steps leading up to him.

When the invaders stopped to pick it up, Steve attempted to escape by the rear window, but was caught. Steve, who spoke Spanish, assured them he would write checks for all those who failed to get cash.

Some grumbled the checks might not be good. Steve, however, was fortunate that among the bandidos was a former employee of his, Eligio Hernandez, who had cowboyed for Uncle Steve. Eligio had lived with a common-law wife at the time and one day got into an argument and shot her dead. When summoned to the scene, Steve gave Hernandez what pay he had coming, explaining that the sheriff's office was in Deming, a day's ride on a horse, and another day for the sheriff's return, pointing out this gave Hernandez 48 hours to disappear. This is exactly what Eligio did, by changing his name to Carlos Dominguez and returning to Mexico to avoid arrest.[4]

Dominguez recognized his previous benefactor, and returned the favor. He told his fellow Villistas that Uncle Steve Birchfield's checks were always good, so they took these pieces of paper made out for demanded sums in lieu of killing him. Other guests were not so fortunate. William Ritchie, hotel manager, whose wife and daughters had been lowered to safety by the improvised rope, was taken to the street with a number of others and shot to death.[5] Others to lose their lives in similar fashion were Dr. H. M. Hart, a veterinarian who was in Columbus to inspect livestock crossing into the U.S. from Mexico, and John Walker, who had come to see about operating some of the cars in Arthur Evans' charter car and taxi service out of his Ford garage.[6]

Villista Colonels Vargas and Ortiz were seeking bigger game. They wanted Sam Ravel, owner of the largest store in Columbus. These two men had been informed by their spies as to the location of the Ravel residence, located a few doors west of the Deming highway. After battering down the door, they found only a frightened 12-year-old boy, Arthur, Sam's brother. The middle brother, Louie, had remained overnight in the store and then hid under a stack of cowhides upon hearing the approach of the Villistas.

The two Villa officers learned from Arthur that Sam had gone to El Paso to have a sinus condition treated there at Hotel Dieu Hospital, then they forced Arthur to accompany them to the Ravel store, where they ordered Arthur to open the combination safe. Arthur convinced them he didn't know the combination, so they left without learning the whereabouts of Louie.[7]

Two doors west of the Ravel store was the *Courier* weekly newspaper office, where Susan Parks, wife of the editor, remained the night of the raid with her baby daughter, Gwen. Susan was temporarily operating the telephone switchboard after a fire destroyed the original telephone building and the equipment was moved to the *Courier* office until new quarters were completed.

When the shooting started, Susan picked up her six-month-old daughter and backed away from the window into the darkness, holding her hand over the mouth of her baby, so her cries could not be heard. At the first lull, Susan opened the line to Deming, instructing the operator there: "Get help and come quick to Columbus—Mexicans are burning and looting the town." She then pulled the connection and again

A BUSINESS BLOCK IN COLUMBUS, N.M., before the raid. The **Courier,** *Columbus's weekly newspaper, ceased publication shortly after the raid.*

retreated into the deep shadows.

The Deming operator, surprised, didn't understand the instructions, so she rang back. This ring attracted another sombreroed figure who fired at the noise, splintering the window glass. Susie crawled to the switchboard, rang Deming back and instructed them not to call again: "Every-time this rings, somebody shoots," she said. "I'll keep the line open. Just wait there, but don't ring!"[8] Mrs. Parks sat by the switchboard throughout the raid, feeding information to Deming as to its progress, while the N.M. National Guard was dispatched to the scene.

About one block west on Broadway was the Lemmon and Romney store, with five 50-gallon drums of gasoline sitting outside. One of these was struck by a bullet and exploded. Juan Favela watched as it flew about 100 feet through the air to land on the Commercial Hotel across the street, dousing it with blazing gas. Soon the entire structure was ablaze, lighting up the center of town.[9]

James Dean, owner of the town's largest grocery, arose upon hearing the firing, dressed and walked rapidly to his store, where he was attacked by a raider and disemboweled with a machete. Dean's son, Edwin, came looking for his father, but didn't reach the grocery. He came across Lt. Castleman and his men at the Broadway intersection and stopped to help remove three injured men to the office of Dr. Dabney, nearby. One of the injured was Private Jesse P.

Taylor, who succumbed the next day.

It is generally understood that the Villistas did most of the shooting and Columbus residents and U.S. soldiers most of the dying, but this is not so. Ten civilians—including one woman—and eight soldiers lost their lives, while only two civilians and two soldiers were wounded. More than 200 Villistas were killed and many more injured. Exact figures are not available. There was no official roster, but the Mexican dead numbered probably more than 200, because the Villistas were caught in a cross-fire while concentrated in a downtown area illuminated by a flaming hotel, a huge frame building that blazed throughout most of the fighting.

*Lt. James P. Castleman, officer the day
Pancho Villa raided.*

More than 200 Villista soldiers were shot to death during the raid on Columbus. Most of them were placed in piles, soaked with gasoline and burned on the spot.

The morning after Villa's raid, a soldier seeks salvage from remains of the Commercial Hotel.

Stretched across the northeast corner of the main town square were the men under Lt. Castleman, 16 sharpshooters, in total darkness firing at human targets made conspicuous by a blazing light. Diagonally, in the opposite direction, was Lt. Lucas and the four machine guns blasting away at a foe concentrated in the center.

Lt. Lucas wrote in his official report: "As a matter of fact, the four machineguns used up about five-thousand rounds apiece in the hour-and-a-half they were in action."[10] That means a total of 20,000 rounds of ammunition was fired into the concentrated ranks of about 500 Mexican invaders who were operating in the northern half of one village block.

This shooting got too much for Pablo Lopez, Villa's second in command. Pablo ordered the bugler to blow retreat, then he ran for his horse and attempted to make his getaway down Broadway. Just as he was turning near the street leading to the depot a bullet entered his right hip and came out his left, knocking the officer off his horse. Lopez was picked up by a soldier named Baez, who carried him back into Mexico.[11]

Jesus Carreon helped his father drive more than a hundred head of mules out of Mexico to Columbus the day before Villa raided. Carreon remained in Columbus, prospered in the grocery business and became mayor.

VILLA RAIDS THE TOWN. Pancho Villa and his rough-and-ready Villista soldiers appeared like this to residents of small towns along the Mexican border who were unfortunate enough to get in his path. What induced him to raid Columbus, N.M.? Could it have been our own government?

The raid was over by the time the sun came fully up, but there was still more violence. Mr. and Mrs. John J. Moore thought their homestead, located three miles southwest of Columbus, was safe, only to learn they were in the direct line of retreat.

At dawn, a uniformed man in a cape and mounted on a white horse stopped in front of their home, accompanied by 20 or more soldiers (among whom was Martin Lopez) and they dismounted. The commander in white, a Colonel Cervantes, walked to Moore's well to determine if there was water for their horses. The colonel was spotted by Mr. Moore, who advised his wife, "We'd better get in the dining room." A short time later they heard footsteps on their porch.[12]

Moore answered a knock at the door, and it was Cervantes, who inquired if the Moores were hiding Sam Ravel. Moore replied they were not, and then the caped man asked that they give him whatever valuables they had in the house, whereupon Moore grabbed a rifle he kept near the front door and forced his way past the officer. He was shot instantly, but staggered several yards, firing his gun wildly.

Mrs. Moore, meanwhile ran out a rear door and hid in their garage, where she was discovered by Villistas and ran, but was shot in the leg. She hid under some mesquite after running into the yard, explaining later she knew she would be killed if she lay out in the open. At the sound of approaching horses, Mrs. Moore waved her handkerchief at Captain Rudolph Smyser, who halted his men and went to her, sending one of his men back for an ambulance.

Meanwhile, Jack Breen—a cowboy, rancher and deputy sheriff—arrived in Columbus and joined a group of residents who were saddling up to give chase, but they were ordered by Colonel H. J. Slocum, the commandant, not to do so.[13]

"You could hear them cocking their revolvers in defiance of the Colonel's order," Breen said, and they mounted in defiance and rode off, under the leadership of Buck Chadborn and Jolly Garner, two line-riders. They soon encountered the messenger asking for an ambulance, and Deputy Breen volunteered to accompany it to the Moore homestead.

Mrs. Maude Medders, meanwhile, was retreating with the

Col. Herbert J. Slocum was in command of the Army base at Columbus when the raid occurred.

Villa forces toward the border. Once there, Pancho asked if she would like to return home. She asked if he meant to her U.S. home, or the one in Mexico. Pancho replied to the United States, and she replied, "I sure do." She got off her horse and began walking back north, toward Columbus.[14]

Within minutes, Maude arrived at the Moore homestead, where she first discovered the body of Mr. Moore. She then came upon Mrs. Moore hiding in the mesquite. She brought her water from the well and remained with the injured woman until Deputy Breen arrived with the ambulance.[15]

1. Lt. John Lucas report, *Chasing Villa*, p. 51.

2. Ibid.

3. Ibid., p. 52.

4. Jack Breen, Luna County Deputy Sheriff who investigated the crime, interview with author, 1960, Columbus, N.M.

5. Breen interview.

6. Daniel (Buck) Chadborn, interview with author, Deming, June 1960.

7. Arthur and Louis Ravel, interview with author, July 20, 1960, at their Albuquerque feed store.

8. Susan Parks' son, Jim, interview with mother, March 22, 1971, taped.

9. Juan Favela, Diamond A's foreman, interview with author, 1960.

10. Tompkins, *Chasing Villa*, p. 52.

11. Jesus Maria Lopez, brother of Pablo, interview with author at Lopez's home at El Charco, Chi., March 1960.

12. Mrs. John Moore, testimony before Senator A. B. Fall's sub-committee, Vol. 2, pp. 956-67, at hearing presided over by Lt. Henry O. Flipper, Fall's administrative assistant.

13. Breen, interview with author.

14. Maude Medders (later to marry a man named Wright), interview with author at her ranch home near Mountainaire, N.M., May 1960.

15. Maude Medders, testimony before Senator A. B. Fall's Senate sub-committee, Vol. 2, pp. 267-8.

They were all involved in the Columbus raid. Jack Breen (seated at far left) was host to other prominent figures in the Columbus raid: Juan Favela (seated in center), Johnny Wright (standing), and his mother Maude who rode with Villa into Columbus. Photo taken when the Pancho Villa Park was dedicated in Columbus.

The raid on Columbus caused one of the first military air bases in the Southwest to be established there to accommodate a squadron of Curtis Jennies, which were used by the U.S. Army in the expedition later mounted against Pancho Villa in his retreat into Mexico.

CHAPTER XIV
Secrets Will Out
(A Haunting Memory)

Pancho Villa's raid on Columbus, N.M., ravaged the lives of most of the people then living there, but it provided a financial boon to at least one—Arthur J. Evans, the Ford dealer and owner of the town's only taxi company and auto charter service. Arthur's business thrived as a result of the attack, but secrets remaining in its wake haunted Arthur to the very day of his death, October 20, 1975, when he was 75 years old.

Arthur's great adventure opened on March 3, 1916, six days before the raid, when the noon train from El Paso arrived at the depot and discharged a 31-year-old Associated Press correspondent, George L. Seese, accompanied by his 16-year-old recent bride. The couple hired Arthur's taxi at the depot and asked the driver to take them to "the town's best boarding house."

"There was only one boarding house then," Arthur explained a half-century later, agreeing to an interview on the stipulation it would not be published—attributable to him— during his lifetime. He still feared reprisal.[1]

"The boarding house was operated by Mr. and Mrs. E. A. Singer," he explained, "and the Seeses roomed and boarded there for about a week." This was corroborated when the Singers visited Columbus in July 1962.[2]

Seese usually spent his mornings walking about Columbus, and was often seen by Evans ascending Coots Hill, where he would peer off into Mexico, about two miles to the south, with binoculars. Evans' home was located at the foot of Coots Hill and members of his family remarked about this peculiar habit.[3]

On the morning of Wednesday, March 8, Seese went to the Western Union counter at the Columbus depot and sent a telegram to the El Paso AP office, directing them to send a special telegrapher, E. A. Van Camp, to the office of the Newman Investment Company, at the corner of San Antonio and El Paso streets. There he was to pick up a package

Arthur Evans as he appeared at the time of the raid while operating the taxi and charter car service, as well as running a Ford garage.

addressed to Seese and was to bring it with him on the 10:30 train that night from El Paso, arriving in Colum¹ us shortly before midnight. Seese explained he anticipated sending an important story for the AP the next day and needed a special telegrapher.

This message was handed to the regular Western Union operator, W. S. Murphy, who remonstrated to Seese, declaring that he—Murphy—was capable of sending any story Seese might write or dictate, but Seese assured him that an experienced AP telegrapher was imperative for a story of its length and importance.[4]

Van Camp, following instructions, arrived on the train that Wednesday night, March 8, and was met at the depot by Seese, who had arranged for a room for Van Camp at the Commercial Hotel.

After the first sound of shooting, shortly after 4 A.M., March 9, Seese arrived at the Commercial Hotel, aroused

Van Camp, and they rushed to the train depot, bashed in the door, and began sending out the story of the Columbus raid, telling the story of how less than 50 U.S. soldiers defended the village against a force of more than 500 Mexican Villistas.

This story thrilled the world, but had even a greater effect on its author, for it established the whereabouts of Seese and his new bride, for the latter's father was particularly interested since he learned that Seese was already married to a woman in New York state and he had never been divorced. He notified Luna County authorities they had a bigamist in their midst and departed for Columbus, where it was said he intended to shoot Seese.[5]

Seese learned of this disturbing development almost immediately, probably through the Luna County Sheriff's office, according to Evans, and the AP man departed immediately for Canada, taking his bride with him.

Before departing, Seese turned the paper-wrapped bundle over to Van Camp, explaining that it contained money and instructed him to show up at 9 A.M., Sunday, March 12, at Evans' garage, explaining a car had been ordered and paid for

Associated Press Correspondent George Seese roomed with these people while waiting in Columbus for the Villa raid. From left, Mrs. E. A. Skinner and Mr. Skinner, who owned the boarding house, and their daughter, Miriam Hutchinson Skinner, with Mrs. Charles Birchfield, of prominent Columbus family.

that would drive him to a scheduled rendezvous with Pancho Villa at Lake Guzman, about 50 miles south of Columbus. Once there, he was to turn the $80,000 in big U.S. bills over to Villa.[6]

Arthur Evans said he and Van Camp arrived at Laguna Guzman before Villa, but that Pancho was only a few minutes late and was accompanied by two men, all on horseback. The package was given to a Villa assistant, his fiscal agent, who counted the bills hurriedly and then the three rode off from whence they came.

While they were driving back to Columbus, Van Camp told Evans what he knew of the transaction, and of Seese's trouble with his bride. Evans later said he assumed Van Camp took a train back to Chicago, his home base. Attempts to locate him there years later through the AP failed.

Arthur Evans as he appeared in the 1920s at Columbus.

Van Camp did return to Columbus at least one more time, however, and had his picture taken there by Arthur Evans, who was also invited to this reunion of the people involved in the secret payoff, including Lieutenant John Lucas, hero of the defense of the town against the Villistas.

Evans said he was not positive, but suspected this second meeting resulted from demands from Villa for $50,000 additional to maintain his silence about the deal, and government authorities wanted the money to be delivered to the retired bandit by the same people who dealt with him initially. Evans added, however, that additional money was not paid in his opinion. The only participant in this second meeting who was not present at the first one was Tom Mahoney, who became city editor of the El Paso *Post* at age 22, the youngest in the Scripps-Howard organization.

"George Seese got fired," Mahoney wrote in a letter to the author, dated October 4, 1962, "by the AP for being involved in a bigamy case, or at least involving a girl on the border which made it desirable for him to depart elsewhere. Years later he became editor or publisher of a small paper in Middletown, N.Y. Some years before he died (in 1954) I wrote him saying that I wanted to do a real definitive story of the affair. He replied with a plea that I leave him out of the story as it would *destroy him*. (Mahoney's emphasis). I did not pursue the project."

The important historical result from the raid, however, remains clear. That is, the United States could not have entered World War I on the side of the Allies so quickly had not Pancho Villa first raided Columbus.

Just six days after the raid, General John J. Pershing, commander at Fort Bliss in El Paso, put together forces for a punitive expedition into Mexico, based at Columbus. His true mission, however, was to determine how much of an army he really had.

Pershing's command was called a "punitive expedition" for the first time in his general orders, No. 1, March 14, 1916, and specified his forces were comprised of the 5th, 7th, 10th, 11th and 13th Cavalry Regiments; Batteries B and C, 6th Field Artillery; 6th and 16th Cavalry Regiments; one machine-gun troop; First Aero Squadron; Companies E and H, Second

Battalion of Engineers; Field Hospital No. 7; and an ambulance company.

Pershing's orders were "to pursue" and "disperse" the Villistas. He was not ordered to "capture" Pancho Villa. In essence, the raid provided a proper excuse to call out our various state militias and National Guard units in an effort to determine their numbers and state of preparedness.

President Wilson had asked several governors to call out their guard units to determine their size and quality, but the governors refused, asking that the President give them an "excuse" for such an unpopular act. Thus the stage was set for a raid by Pancho Villa against Columbus, to provide a reason to call out the guard militia. By July 31, 1916, 110,957 officers and enlisted men had flocked to the border, with an additional 40,139 guardsmen gathered in various mobilization camps, the nucleus of our needed army.[7]

This was the first time actual figures have been available to the President or others to determine the number of various militia units and their individual numbers had been determined. The United States had virtually no standing army and Villa's raid at Columbus was imperative to provide an incident which would give us preparedness. The raid propelled Congress to pass a National Defense Act of 1916, allowing state militia units to pass into federal service.

Pershing set up his first headquarters at Casas Grandes, where he divided the area of operation into six districts: Namiquipa, 10th Cavalry; Guerrero, 7th Cavalry; Bustillos, 13th Cavalry; Satevo, 5th Cavalry; and the 11th Cavalry at San Borja.[8]

Pershing's regular army forces numbered only a few thousand. His job was not to win any wars, or capture Villa, but it was to manage what troops he had in the field and to determine their state of preparedness. Later Congress would pass a national conscription act to supply men for our huge undertaking in joining our allies in the European war then raging in Europe.

The expedition gave the army an opportunity to try out its supply system. Congress appropriated millions of dollars to work on this problem alone. White and Quad trucks were purchased, repaired and serviced to carry supplies and ordnance to American forces in Mexico, but they proved inadequate in such terrain, so mules replaced them.

Meanwhile, Columbus grew from three hundred people to ten thousand. A large number of civilians were needed to service and repair the 600 or so trucks bringing in troop supplies, plus a number of mechanics to keep the Aero squadron flying. There were also arms smugglers, pimps, stick-up men, murderers, German and Mexican spies and American spies to watch them. There were taxi drivers, railroad men, preachers, tailors, merchants and barbers. There were cowboys, truck drivers, delivery boys, icemen and just plain people who could do a little of almost anything.

A fancy-dressed little Negro man also showed up. Whenever anybody asked his name, he replied, "Call me Buck-'n'-a-half," which was shortened to Buckenahalf. Nobody knows to this day of another name. He stirred a mild riffle of interest when he went to the northeast end of town and asked the rent being asked for a two-room adobe shack. Since he was black, they told him twice as much as they intended to ask.

"It'll be $200 a month," the owner said, and his mouth got dry when he saw Buckenahalf pull out a large roll and count off ten $20 gold certificates.

"It's all right iffen I jes put another door to this here room right here, ain't it?" asked Buckenahalf. "Iffen I pay for it my own self?"

"Ya kin put a doorway into hell as long as you pay that $200 every month," replied the owner.[9]

Buckenahalf put in another door, so that he had him a two-room house with doors on the east and on the west, then he painted the front room all purple, trimmed in gold, and put yellow satin drapes at the windows.

One day a huge crate came in at the depot and Buckenahalf hired young Jesus Carreon to pick it up for him, which Jesus did in his model T flatbed.

Jesus later became mayor of Columbus, was mayor until the day he died in the 1970s, and was called just plain Sus. He was real easy going, so easy to get along with that a wag climbed up on our water tower and painted in big, red letters: JESUS RUNS OUR TOWN!

Anyway, all this took place when Sus was just a boy, about

the time he helped his father run a hundred head of mules up to Columbus from their ranch down in Chihuahua so Pancho Villa couldn't steal them. He never thought about being mayor in those days. He just ran a delivery truck and sometimes drove a taxi or charter car for Arthur Evans. He also delivered ice from the ice house.

This one day, Jesus picked up a crate and hauled it out to Buckenahalf's two-room adobe and was the first person in Columbus who had a close look at the remodeled place. Sus helped the Negro open the crate and assemble a huge brass bed inside. It was the most magnificent brass bed in all of New Mexico, Sus explained later, all worked back and forth with lacy brass convoluted designs, and knobs, with angels blowing trumpets and strumming harps on the bedposts.

Buckenahalf rode back to the center of town with Sus and went over to Ravel's General Store, where he bought a big washtub. The last Sus saw of him that day, he was walking toward his "palace" with the tub over his head.

Standup electric fans with eight-inch blades were unusual in this part of the country in 1916. At Powers' Drug Store they had a big wooden-blade fan circulating slow and revolving over the soda counter, but regular electric fans were not a usual item. There was a good reason, too, for Dick Doby had been running the gas generator for months at the Onyx Movie House and not too many places were wired for electricity. So, when Jesus picked up this big fan from back East at the depot, he was puzzled, but delivered it without asking any questions.

Buckenahalf took the fan out of the box and placed it on a little half-shelf just below the window of the front room and turned it on to try the fan out. When it was going real good, he got down on his knees and stuck his face up to the breeze, closed his eyes and let her blow, with a real big smile on his face. Then he got up and put the washtub between the fan and the bed.

"You deliver ice from the icehouse, don't you?" asked Buckenahalf.

"You bet," replied Sus.

"Then starting next Saturday morning," instructed Buckenahalf, I want you to bring 25 pounds of ice here in a single chunk twice a day—once at 10 in the morning, and again at 2 in the afternoon. Jesus loaded up a 25-pound chunk of ice on his model T and chugged out toward Hacienda Buckenahalf. As he drove around the mesquite bush in front, Jesus noticed Buckenahalf standing on the stoop at the west entrance. He motioned Jesus to bring the ice.

Jesus put the piece of burlap over his back and hefted the ice onto his shoulder, then headed for the door. For the first time, he noticed a sign above that said: ART MUSEUM. Through this door he went, swung around the washtub and plopped the chunk of ice there, in front of the fan. As he swung downward with the ice, he thought he saw a figure in the bed, but the ice obstructed his view. After dropping the ice into the tub, Jesus looked back over his shoulder to see who—or what—it was in that fancy brass bed.

Jesus started with his eyes at the foot of the bed and worked up, taking in every minute detail. Frozen, he stood silently and almost breathlessly in the center of the room and stared. This time his eyes moved from the trumpeting angels at the head of the bed back to the harpists at the foot. Jesus sucked air and fell on his hands and knees, placing his face directly in front of the fan, and allowed the refreshing breezes to blow over his feverish forehead. For a few seconds he fumbled around as though he couldn't pick up the burlap bag. Finally he got it and stumbled backwards out of the doorway. He sat on the ground a few moments, thinking. Then he rose and walked around the back of the house and approached Buckenahalf on the other side.

"Buckenahalf," he said, "there's a girl in there in that bed."

"Tha's right," said Buckenahalf.

"She...she...she's naked!"

"That she is," agreed Buckenahalf.

"She didn't even look up when I delivered the ice in there," said Jesus.

"That's the idea," said Buckenahalf. "She ain't s'posed to look at you. You're supposed to look at her."

"I did," said Jesus.

"Whatcha think?"

"That's the prettiest woman I ever saw in my whole life— even in pictures, drawn, or anything. She's the prettiest."

Buckenahalf's face broke into a large and beatific grin, "She sure is, ain't she?" he said.

"Cheengow!" exclaimed Jesus. "She is perfect in every way. Her face, everything. She's perfect."

"That's what we mean," said Buckenahalf expansively, as he pointed a bony finger at the ART MUSEUM sign, "when we say, 'fine art'."

What is she with that yellow-gold color?" asked Jesus, "a mulatto?"

"Nope," said Buckenahalf, "she's what you call a octoroon, boy."

"What's that mean?" asked Jesus, for there were few Negroes in the Southwest, so few that esoteric expressions and gradations of color had not entered the language.

"Means she's one-eighth Negro," said Buckenahalf, smiling. "And where she comes from they still call anybody who is just one-eighth Negro a nigger. But do you know," he continued wickedly, lifting an eyebrow, "I ain't never heard nobody... ever...ever...call that golden gal in there a nigger, 'cause after they take one look at her, they go 'round saying words like 'deevine!' and like 'exquiseet'!"

"What do just people call her?" asked Jesus.

"Pretty Baby," replied Buckenahalf.

And Pretty Baby it was, all the time the Army and all the folks were in Columbus. Pretty Baby became the thing to see if you visited Columbus. Pretty Baby was like the Eiffel Tower in Paris, the Taj Mahal in India, the Sphinx in Egypt, the Tower of London. But she shone above them all as the main attraction in Buckenahalf's ART MUSEUM.

Art connoisseurs came from all over to drink in her breathtaking beauty. Rapturously, they proclaimed that she beat all, even Mona Lisa. Art, you might say, became furiously popular, as everybody in the various infantry units, the cavalry, the artillery—just everybody—became connoisseurs of real live art, the kind that beat all. They supported the museum more magnificently than ever one had been supported in New York, or Paris, or Rome, or Suez. The patrons literally fought to donate a dollar-and-a-half it cost at the door. Old Buckenahalf just stood at the entrance and a steady stream of soldiers—black and white, Chinese and

Apache, Anglo and French, Spanish and Alaskan or Hawaiian and anything in between—trooped up, gave their money and marched into the east entrance of the art palace and out the west door.

They had to keep moving as they gazed at the gold-trimmed-in-black art treasure that lay stretched out there before them. For the most part, it was before they had inspected all the details. This, of course, necessitated another trip and produced another Buck-'n'-a-half.

"Y'all keep moving in there," he would shout every now and then, as he stuck his head in the door, "or we'll have to cut you all off iffen you don't keep moving. Now, jes keep going."

The ones behind would push the ones in front and keep the line moving forward, so they couldn't get "cut off."

And the girl, what was she like?

"How do you describe perfect?" the late Columbus Mayor Jesus V. Carreon answered with a question. "She was perfection. I never seen anything even near as pretty since. No, there was only one Pretty Baby and I never hope to see another."

Jesus explained that the oddest part was how nonchalant Pretty Baby was. How unaffected. She would just lie there, naked, and read a book, or a magazine, or sleep, or look at the ceiling and do nothing at all, not even look at her admirers. The electric fan forced a draft across the ice, and this blew on her and kept her cool and comfortable, even in 100-degree summer temperatures. The moisture seemed to cover her like dew on her raven hair and eyebrows, over her purple eyes.

New soldiers wouldn't be in Columbus long before somebody would ask, 'Dja see Pretty Baby yet?" and if the answer was no, the newcomer was hustled over to the art palace and given a good look at the most precious art treasure in this whole part of the Southwest.

Buckenahalf and Pretty Baby surely grew tremendously wealthy, but you couldn't tell it. They spent little, bought little. Some food, books, magazines—and ice. They did buy six lots and planned to build a new art palace, but when the troops moved out, the bubble burst.

So, they moved on.

Nobody knew where. Just disappeared as mysteriously as

they came. Buckenahalf wore the same old black derby. And Pretty Baby...well, she looked best in nothing at all, and that didn't cost anything.

What might be considered peculiar to some is that Pretty Baby—in no sense whatsoever—was a prostitute—that is, in the ordinary sense of the word. There were houses of prostitution in Columbus when the Army was there, too, but that was a different thing.

One time when this question arose in the Pancho Villa Cantina, Mayor Jesus said, "No sir, I am sure no man in the whole world ever slept with Pretty Baby."

Ramon Gutierrez, the bartender, was a small boy when Pretty Baby was there, but he remembered her.

"What did you say she was? asked Ramon. "A Vinegaroon, or something?"

"I said an octoroon," explained the mayor, a little testily.

"Hm," said Ramon, "I woulda swore she was a Swede."

1. Arthur J. Evans, interview with author, one of several during 1960-61.

2. Mr. and Mrs. E. A. Singer, interview with author, July, 1962, at Columbus for story appearing in *The Southwesterner*, a historical monthly.

3. Evans, interview with author, 1960.

4. W. S. Murphy, testimony before the A. B. Fall Senate hearing, 1916.

5. Arthur Evans, interview with author, 1961.

6. Details of this procedure were gone over in several interviews with Evans in 1960-61, by author.

7. Tompkins, *Chasing Villa*, p. 228.

8. Colonel H. A. Toulman, Jr., *With Pershing in Mexico*, Military Publishing Company, Harrisburg, PA, 1935, p. 114.

9. Jesus Carreon, Mayor of Columbus, interview with author, 1960.

CHAPTER XV
Was It Kosher What Lottie Did?
(A Lotta Dinero Comes High)

When she first arrived in New Mexico, she was known as Lottie Deno, but after out-dealing the sharpest gamblers in the Southwest, she was honored with the sobriquet "Lotta Dinero," which is border Spanish for "lots of money."

She was barely five-foot-three and said she was born in Warsaw, Kentucky, April 21, 1844, of a prominent family. She never divulged its name, but did boast her father was a Kentucky State Legislator and owned a racing stable. Lottie also told how, as a young girl, she accompanied her father to Europe on a business trip.[1]

Gallatin County, Ky., did not keep birth records when Lottie was born, and U.S. census records for 1850 and 1860 list no Lotties or Charlottes of the proper age. A Charlotte is listed in 1850, the 20-year-old wife of a cooper named Headrich Hall, and in the 1860 census is a Charlotte, 22, wife of a laborer, W. Craxton, which doesn't fit either.

Charlotte's death certificate gives her name as Lottie Thurmond, with a long string of "Don't know" answers to questions concerning her family, maiden name of her mother, or her father's family name. Her official identification is "widow of Frank Thurmond," who died in 1908.

Lottie left a third of her estate to her undertaker, J. A. Mahoney, and the balance to Sigmund Lindauer, a Deming merchant and friend over the years, and Mrs. Allie Bell Stecker, "share and share alike."[2]

Much earlier, Lottie was so notorious and her adventures so thrilling they were fictionalized by Alfred Henry Lewis for *Cosmopolitan* magazine in the late 1890s, then made into three books.[3]

Lottie is best remembered in Deming, N.M., as a church and social leader who taught in the Episcopalian Sunday School and who organized the Golden Gossip Club, a group of women who met weekly to knit, gossip and socialize. It is probable she was also the first Jew to teach in the Episcopal

*Lottie Deno as she appeared during her
days as a "desperate" woman.*

Sunday School.

Lottie's professional career began in the gambling halls of
New Orleans, later in San Antonio and she arrived in Fort
Griffin, Texas, in 1876, when it was a frontier town loaded

with rich buffalo hunters, Indians and soldiers. She was a professional gambler and worked for the Bee Hive, a gambling joint owned by an Irishman named John Shaunessey and run by a man named Fogarty.[4]

It was here one night two gamblers, known as Monte Bill and Smokey Joe, had a gun battle in front of her, clearing out the other customers with the zing and bang of bullets across the gaming table. When it was over, Lottie was shuffling cards, with the bodies of Joe and Bill lying on each side of her. When Sheriff Cruger arrived, he remarked at Lottie's coolness under fire.

"Why didn't you vamoose?" he asked, and Lottie replied, "It was too late."

"I don't believe I would have wanted to take my chances in that scrimmage," the sheriff admitted, and Lottie replied, "Perhaps not, but you aren't a desperate woman."[5]

Lottie was married to a quick-tempered, half-breed Cherokee, ex-Confederate soldier named Frank Thurmond, a knife-fighter who carried a 13-inch Bowie knife at all times.[6] The couple had previously resided in San Antonio, where her husband and his brother, Bob, operated and owned the Cosmopolitan Saloon, where Lottie was both a dealer and look-out. Lottie confided to Herman Lindauer, a Deming merchant, that her husband had chopped a man to death in a knife fight. She turned over to her husband all their cash and valuables so he could flee from prosecution to Mexico.

Later, Thurmond met Lottie and they proceeded to Silver City, N.M., and because that was not yet a state, he felt he might be safe from prosecution. They arrived in Silver City with a small leather trunk filled with $30,000 in silver coins.[7]

When gold and silver strikes were made at Kingston, the Thurmonds sold their gambling and dance hall in Silver City, to open a casino and bar in the midst of the new field. Soon the rich strike also attracted two Irishmen to the area, John and Edward Bradley, of Johnstown, Pa. They were destined to become the aristocrats of American gambling, plus world-famous Kentucky thoroughbred horse breeders. Colonel Ed Bradley was the first owner and breeder whose horses ran first and second in two different Kentucky Derbys.

Sigmund Lindauer's mercantile store was located at nearby

Frank Thurmond, Lottie's gambler husband, in photograph taken at a family outing near Deming in the 1880s.

Georgetown, so he and the Thurmonds became close friends, perhaps because both Sig and Lottie were of the Jewish faith. The Thurmonds sold their gambling hall at Kingston, while Lindauer sold his mercantile store at Georgetown and opened another in Deming.

The Thurmonds settled down to an orderly, if prosaic, life in Deming, where they were often visited by George Hearst, who owned gold and silver mines in the area. His son, William Randolph, was publisher of *Cosmopolitan* magazine. At the elder Hearst's suggestion, William Randolph sent Alfred Henry Lewis to Deming for lengthy visits to write about the Thurmonds. He was accompanied by Frederick Remington, who illustrated the stories.

During weeks of interviews, Lottie and Frank told of their earlier adventures, and the stories began appearing in *Cosmopolitan* as fiction, with Lottie and Frank disguised as Faro Nell and Cherokee Hall, living in a place called Wolfville. Herman Lindauer, son of Sigmund, described Thurmond as "part Cherokee and a deadly knife fighter."[8] Herman observed that Frank eagerly read the stories about himself and Lottie as fast as they came out in *Cosmopolitan,* claiming "They are the only true and authentic stories about the Southwest."

Among these yarns was a fictionalized account of an attempt by Doc Holliday to take over the Thurmond's gambling casino. He put up $30,000 in a poker game in which he would win either the gambling hall, or Thurmond would take his $30,000. It was stated at Lottie's insistence that if Doc should break Frank, he must then take on "Nell" and beat her before he could take over their establishment.

Lottie had $30,000 of her own money for this venture and Doc Holliday agreed to the terms.

Cherokee allows Holliday to set the limit and Doc replies, "I'll jest natcherly take every resk of splits an' put ten thousand in the pot, coppered; then ten thousand on the big squar', and ten thousand, coppered, on high kyard."

Three cards were turned and Holliday won thirty thousand dollars. He lost ten back on high card, then bet twenty thousand and won, breaking Cherokee.

"An' now you got to break me," Nell tells Holliday, "an' the limit retreats to an even hundred dollars."

Nell manages to win back the forty-thousand and tells Holliday she's willing to play no limit, inviting him, as Alfred Henry Lewis puts it, "to go as far as you like—the bridle's off the horse."

Holiday makes the same three bets he made to break Cherokee, but this time the bank wins, and Holliday is broke.

"The drinks is on me," says Nell. "See what the house will have."

The story is said to be a fairly accurate account of an actual encounter with Holliday, but few people in Deming could believe that Faro Nell and Charlotte Thurmond were the same, not that sweet old lady who organized the Golden

Mrs. Frank Thurmond, as Lottie was known when this photograph was taken on the porch of her home, is seated at far left with members of the Deming Golden Gossip Club.

Gossip Club.

According to Herman, Lottie was Jewish, as were the Lindauers, and she spent her last days with that family, while his father, Sigmund, was still living and before they sat Kaddish (Jewish prayer for the dead) over Lottie's departure from this earth. Herman said that shortly before she died, Lottie complained to him and his father about the vulgar way Lewis had written about her.

"I can't understand," Lottie said shortly before she died, "why he had me speak in such an uneducated and vulgar manner, for you can see that I don't use such disgraceful language."

1. Details of Lottie's life were provided by the late Herman Lindauer, a Deming, N.M. merchant, a close friend.

2. J. Marvin Hunter, *The Story of Lottie Deno*, published by Four Hunters, Bandera, TX, 1959, pp. 192-3.

3. *Wolfville, Wolfville Days*, and *Wolfville Nights*, by Alfred Henry Lewis, published by Frederick Stokes, 1897, and Grosset & Dunlap, NY, 1902.

4. Hunter, *Lottie Deno*, pp. 40-41.

5. Edgar Rye, an eye-witness who wrote of the incident in his book, *The Quirt and Spur*, Conkey Co., Chicago, 1909.

6. Herman Lindauer, interview with author, Deming, 1961.

7. Hunter, *Lottie Deno*, p. 46

8. Herman Lindauer, interview with author, 1961, Deming.

Lottie Deno in her later years at Kingston, New Mexico, with her friend Herman Lindauer.

Index

M

Madero, Emilio 102
Madero, Francisco 100-104, 115
Madero, Raul 115
Mahoney, J. A. 146
Mahoney, Tom 138
Maldonado, Alonzo D. 9, 11
Martin, James 29, 31, 32
Martin, Roy 115-118
Martin, Sherman 107
Marx, Karl 30
Matamoras 14, 59
Maxwell, Pete 71
Mayer, Brantz 15
Maytorena, Jose M. 102
McAdoo, William G. 86
McCarty, Catherine 62-64, 70
McCarty, Henry 56-68, 69-72
McCarty, Michael 62
McClellan, Gen. Geo. B. 40
McCutcheon, John H. 89
McGaw, William, 119, 120
McLean, Dr. James Henry 47, 48
McPherson 36, 38
McSween (lawyer) 66, 68, 69
Medders, Maude 131-132
Mesilla, NM 24, 26, 56, 60, 88
Mexican Military Academy 85
Mexican Springs, NM 35
Mexican War 14, 15
Mexico City 12
Milton, Jeff 77-78
Mimbres River 26
Monte Bill 148
Moore, John J. 131
Moore, William 30-31, 32
Morgan, Emma 72
Morgan, Joseph F. 75
Morton and Baker 66
Mowry, Lt. Sylvester 25
Mullin, Robert N. 68
Murphy, L. G. 66
Murphy, W. S. 135

N

New Mexico 12, 35-46
New Orleans 32, 33
Newman Investment Co. 134
Newman, S. H. 85
Niza, Marcos de 12
Noble, Joan W. 33
Nogales, AZ 85-86, 105
Nogales Herald 86
Nolan, Capt. Nicholas 82
Nordstrom, Capt. Chas. E. 83

O

Obregon, Col. Alvaro 103
O'Brian, Capt. John 19
Ogden, R. B. 30, 32-33
O'Neil, James 25
Orchard, Sadie 89
Ornelas, Tomas 118
Orozco, Pascual 101
Otero, Miguel Antonio 70-71, 76

P

Pacheco, Carlos 85
Paine, Albert B. 31
Parker, Frank W. 72, 88-89, 91
Parks, Susan 125-126
Patagonia, AZ 25
Pennypacker, Col. Galusha 84
Pershing, Gen. John J. 138-139
Pettie, Tom 48
Poe, John 71
Point Isabel 15-17
Pretty Baby 142-145
Pyramid Hill 52
Pyramid Station, NM 35-36

R

Ralston City, NM 35-46, 47-55
Ralston, William C. 38, 40, 41, 45
Ravel, Arthur 125
Ravel, Louis 125
Ravel, Sam 125, 131
Reavis, James 86
Reed, John 107
Remington, Frederick 149
Rhodes, Eugene M. 79
Richards, Dr. John Edward 57
Richards, Edward 59, 60
Richards, Mary 56-61, 64-65, 69
Richards, Ruben 59, 60
Ritchie, William 125
Roberts, George D. 38, 39-40, 41, 43
Roosevelt, Theodore 76-77
Rothschild, House of 41
Ruskin, John 57-58

S

Salisbury, Lord 57
Saltillo, Mexico 17-18, 20, 22
San Antonio, TX 148
San Francisco Bulletin 45
Sanford, J. F. 30
Santa Ana, Gen. 18-19, 20
Santa Ysabel massacre 117
Saylor, George 54

ORDER BLANK

Golden West Publishers

4113 N. Longview Ave. ● Phoenix, AZ 85014

Please ship the following books:

_____ **Arizona Adventure** ($5.00)
_____ **Arizona Cook Book** ($3.50)
_____ **Arizona Hideaways** ($4.50)
_____ **Arizona—Off the Beaten Path** ($4.50)
_____ **Arizona Outdoor Guide** ($5.00)
_____ **Bill Williams Mountain Men** ($5.00)
_____ **California Favorites Cook Book** ($3.50)
_____ **Chili-Lovers' Cook Book** ($3.50)
_____ **Citrus Recipes** ($3.50)
_____ **Cowboy Slang** ($5.00)
_____ **Cowboy Country Cartoons** ($4.50)
_____ **Easy Recipes for the Traveling Cook** ($5.00)
_____ **Easy Recipes for Wild Game** ($6.50)
_____ **Explore Arizona** ($5.00)
_____ **Fools' Gold** ($5.00)
_____ **Ghost Towns in Arizona** ($4.50)
_____ **Ginger Hutton...from the Heart** ($5.00)
_____ **How to Succeed Selling Real Estate** ($3.50)
_____ **In Old Arizona** ($5.00)
_____ **Mexican Desserts** ($6.50)
_____ **Mexican Family Favorites Cook Book** ($5.00)
_____ **The Other Mexico** ($9.00)
_____ **On the Arizona Road** ($5.00)
_____ **Pecan-Lovers' Cook Book** ($5.00)
_____ **Prehistoric Arizona** ($5.00)
_____ **Southwest Saga** ($5.00)
_____ **Sphinx Ranch Date Recipes** ($5.00)

Enclosed is $ _____ (including $1 per
book for postage & handling)

_____
(NAME)

_____
(ADDRESS)

_____
(CITY)   (STATE)   (ZIP)

SOUTHWEST SAGA
—the way it really was!

by WILLIAM C. McGAW
author of SAVAGE SCENE

Books from Golden West Publishers

The Other Mexico—Revel in ancient treasures and modern pleasures with world traveler E. J. Guarino, your host to the myriad museums and archaeological ruins in today's Mexico. 90 full-color photographs, plus maps, site-plans, index. (176 pages)...**$9.00**

Cowboy Country Cartoons—a cartoon excursion through the whimsical west of renowned cowboy cartoonist-sculptor Jim Willoughby. Western humor at its ribald best! (128 pages)...**$4.50**

Southwestern frontier tales more thrilling than fiction. Trimble brings history to life with humor, pathos and irony of pioneer lives: territorial politics, bungled burglaries, shady deals, frontier lawmen, fighting editors, Baron of Arizona, horse and buggy doctors, etc. **In Old Arizona** by Marshall Trimble (160 pages)...**$5.00**

Daring deeds and exploits of Wyatt Earp, Buckey O'Neill, the Rough Riders, Arizona Rangers, cowboys, Power brothers shootout, notorious Tom Horn, Pleasant Valley wars, the Hopi revolt—action-packed true tales of early Arizona! **Arizona Adventure** by Marshall Trimble (160 pages)...**$5.00**

Ride the back trails with modern-day mountain men, as they preserve the memory of Arizona's rugged adventurers of the past. Buckskin-clad, the mountain men stage annual treks from Williams, AZ all the way to Phoenix, AZ and to other destinations. Hilarious anecdotes of hard-riding men. **Bill Williams Mountain Men** by Thomas E. Way (128 pages)...**$5.00**

Books from Golden West Publishers

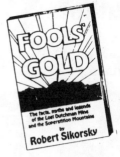

The saga of centuries-old search for Spanish gold and the Lost Dutchman Mine continues. Facts, myths and legends of fabled Superstition Mountains told by a geologist who was there. Mysteries of lost hopes, lost lives—lost gold! *Fools' Gold* by Robert Sikorsky (144 pages) ...*$5.00*

The American cowboy had a way with words! Lingo of the American West, captured in 2000 phrases and expressions—colorful, humorous, earthy, raunchy! Includes horse and cattle terms, rodeo talk, barb wire names, cattle brands. *Cowboy Slang* by "Frosty" Potter, illustrated by Ron Scofield (128 pages)...*$5.00*

Chili cookoff prize-winning recipes and regional favorites! The best of chili cookery, from mild to fiery, with and without beans. Plus a variety of taste-tempting foods made with chile peppers. *Chili-Lovers' Cook Book* by Al and Mildred Fischer (128 pages)...*$3.50 More than 60,000 copies sold!*

More than 200 recipes for Mexican festival desserts, custards, fruits, puddings, gelatines, cakes, pies, cookies, ice creams, sherbets and beverages. The only book of its kind! *Mexican Desserts* by Socorro Munoz Kimble and Irma Serrano Noriega (144 pages)...*$6.50*

More than 250 easy-to-follow homestyle favorite family recipes for tacos, tamales, menudo, enchiladas, burros, salsas, frijoles, chile relleno, carne seca, guacamole and sweet treats! *Mexican Family Favorites Cook Book* by Maria Teresa Bermudez (144 pages)...*$5.00*

Meet the Author

Journalist William Cochran McGaw, an El Paso, Texas, resident, is a respected historian and authority on the Southwest.

Former editor and publisher of the monthly history magazine, *The Southwesterner,* he is a charter member of the Western History Association and a founder of the El Paso corral of The Westerners.

Bill McGaw has been a newspaperman in New Orleans, Indianapolis, Tampa, New York, El Paso and Philadelphia.

He was a motion picture actor at MGM, where he also trained horses. Under contract with the studio as a writer and actor, he played with such stars as Barbara Stanwyck, Clark Gable and Adolph Menjou.

McGaw once owned and lived in a New Mexico ghost town, Mowry City. He organized the Pancho Villa Museum a few miles south of Columbus, NM, and for several years was tour director and press agent for the Royal Lipizzan Stallions.

A former editor and writer for *The Investigator* (a magazine published by columnist Jack Anderson), he has written for various magazines and television. For two years, he had his own prime-time television show on the CBS station KROD in El Paso.

As a columnist for the El Paso *Herald-Post*, he has twice won the Scripps award for the best column in the entire Scripps-Howard chain.

His first book, *Savage Scene, the Life and Times of James Kirker, Frontier King,* has received praise and acclaim from noted historians and writers throughout the West.